THE CATHEDRAL CHURCH OF OXFORD: A DESCRIPTION OF ITS FABRIC AND A BRIEF HISTORY OF THE EPISCOPAL SEE

Published @ 2017 Trieste Publishing Pty Ltd

ISBN 9780649738717

The Cathedral Church of Oxford: A Description of Its Fabric and a Brief History of the Episcopal
See by Percy Dearmer

Edited by Trieste Publishing Pty Ltd.
 Cover @ 2017

www.triestepublishing.com

PERCY DEARMER

THE CATHEDRAL CHURCH OF OXFORD: A DESCRIPTION OF ITS FABRIC AND A BRIEF HISTORY OF THE EPISCOPAL SEE

Trieste

BELL'S CATHEDRAL SERIES:
EDITED BY GLEESON WHITE
AND EDWARD F. STRANGE

OXFORD.

CHRIST CHURCH, FROM THE EAST.

THE CATHEDRAL CHURCH OF
OXFORD
A DESCRIPTION OF ITS FABRIC
AND A BRIEF HISTORY OF THE
EPISCOPAL SEE

BY THE REV. PERCY DEARMER, M.A.

LONDON   GEORGE   BELL   &   SONS   1897

GENERAL PREFACE.

THIS series of monographs has been planned to supply visitors to the great English Cathedrals with accurate and well illustrated guide books at a popular price. The aim of each writer has been to produce a work compiled with sufficient knowledge and scholarship to be of value to the student of archæology and history, and yet not too technical in language for the use of an ordinary visitor or tourist.

To specify all the authorities which have been made use of in each case would be difficult and tedious in this place. But amongst the general sources of information which have been almost invariably found useful are :—firstly, the great county histories, the value of which, especially in questions of genealogy and local records, is generally recognised ; secondly, the numerous papers by experts which appear from time to time in the transactions of the antiquarian and archæological societies ; thirdly, the important documents made accessible in the series issued by the Master of the Rolls ; fourthly, the well-known works of Britton and Willis on the English Cathedrals ; and lastly, the very excellent series of Handbooks to the Cathedrals, originated by the late Mr. John Murray, to which the reader may in most cases be referred for fuller detail, especially in reference to the histories of the respective sees.

GLEESON WHITE.
E. F. STRANGE.
Editors of the Series.

AUTHOR'S PREFACE.

FOR one who has learnt the best of what he knows within Christ Church walls it has been very pleasant to gather these notes of the Cathedral's history and architecture. Moreover, I am less remorseful than I might be at adding to the world's overcrowded library, because certain recent discoveries in the Cathedral have thrown the best of the old books out of date, and made it necessary for some one to weave together the older and the later knowledge. My indebtedness, therefore, is not only to former labourers in this field, but especially to the author of these discoveries, Mr J. Park Harrison, who roused my enthusiasm in the old days, and now has most generously helped me with his advice, and allowed me to incorporate in these chapters the substance of his own papers. To these pamphlets I would refer any who wish to go to the fountain-head for the account of the investigations, and especially I may mention two: "The Pre-Norman Date of the Choir and some of the Stone-work of Oxford Cathedral," and the "Account of the Discovery of the Remains of three Apses at Oxford Cathedral" (Oxford: Frowde, 24 and 23 pp.). I must also express my thanks for the kindness and help of Professor York Powell, and of Mr W. Francis, the senior verger, and to Messrs Carl Norman & Co. of Tunbridge Wells, Mr W. Giles, Mr Park Harrison, and Mr R. Phené Spiers, F.R.I.B.A., for the loan of and permission to reproduce various drawings and photographs.

PERCY DEARMER.

CONTENTS.

ILLUSTRATIONS.

P

THE ROOF OF THE NAVE.

(FROM A DRAWING BY R. PHENÉ SPIERS, F.R.I.B.A.)

OXFORD CATHEDRAL.

CHAPTER I.

THE HISTORY OF THE BUILDING.

THE "Cathedral Church of Christ in Oxford" has had a somewhat unfortunate history. Built for the small monastery of
St. Frideswide, with no thought of any ampler destination, it
was in the sixteenth century raised to the rank of a cathedral,
just after it had been reduced in size by the destruction of
half the nave, and sunk out of sight among a mass of college
buildings. Nor was this all the indignity it suffered; for it
had also to do duty as the chapel of the new academic foundation which Wolsey established, and very soon the cathedral
was forgotten in the college chapel. So neglected was it that
Britton wrote at the beginning of the present century—" It is
very common for visitors, and even those of rather refined and
critical minds, to leave Oxford without examining the building
now under notice." A century earlier Browne Willis had been
content to make the astounding observation : " 'Tis truly no
elegant structure."

The first church on this site was that built by St. Frideswide,
"The Lady," as she was afterwards called in Oxford, and her
father Didan, about the year 727. The story of this saint, which
no visitor to her church should omit to read, will be found in
our chapter on the History of the Foundation.

A contemporary of the Venerable Bede, she was one of those
noble and devoted souls who (as Dr. Jessopp reminds us) made
Anglo-Saxon monasticism the brightest spot in the history of

English community-life.   The monks and nuns of that period
were in fact missionaries, who spread the Christian faith among
the half-civilised *pagani*, or country-folk ; and, by the wise
method of planting themselves in remote districts, and quietly
living the gospel they preached, touched the hearts, and won
the souls, of their rough neighbours.   Thus, without the use
of force, without even the exercise of royal authority, says Professor Freeman, the whole of England had, by the time of the
birth of St. Frideswide (c. 700), accepted the Christian faith. ·
But the religion of the country districts must have still been
of a very untutored description ; and St. Frideswide was one of
those who spread in the South, just at the time when Mercia
was the paramount power in England, the finer civilisation
which had already established itself in the North, and produced
kings like Edwin, saints like Aidan, and poets like Caedmon.
Whatever may be the authority of the legends which gathered
about her name, it is certain that she gave up her high estate,
"devoted herself and all her worldly goods to the service of
Christ and her poor brethren," refused the offer of a royal
marriage, escaped the persecutions of her suitor, "and finally
died in the odour of sanctity, blessed by the poor and ignorant
people to whom she had devoted her troubled life."

Of the place where she established the little church, part of
which can still be seen in the walls of the cathedral, Dr. Liddell,
the late Dean, thus writes :—

"Meadows unbroken by human habitations or human
cultivation, a river wandering through them as it listed, unbarred
by locks, or weirs, or mills, the hills down to their margin
clothed in primeval forest.   The bank of gravel which still
slopes down to what we call Christ Church Meadow, offered a
dry and pleasant site ; the river supplied fish for the inmates
of the new convent ; the Trill-mill stream bears testimony by
its name to the fact that its water was in early times, perhaps
the earliest, used to turn the wheel which ground their corn ;
the neighbouring forests supplied abundant wood for fuel, as
well as game for food, and acorns for the swine ; the rich
meadows of the valley furnished pasture to the flocks and herds.
In those days, no doubt, the existence of such a peaceful community exercised a humanising and softening influence over
the rude thanes and their clansmen and serfs, who had as yet
perhaps hardly heard the name of Christ."

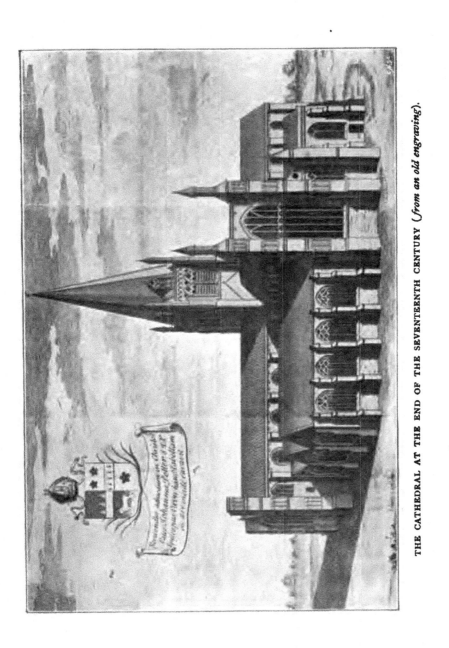

THE CATHEDRAL AT THE END OF THE SEVENTEENTH CENTURY (*from an old engraving*).

Our next glimpse of the church is a terrible one. Despairing of beating back the Danes, Ethelred the Unready gave the mad and treacherous order for the Massacre of St. Brice's Day, 1002. ".Urged by secret orders from the king," says Mr. J. R. Green, "the West Saxons rose on St. Brice's Day, and pitilessly massacred the Danes scattered defencelessly among them. The tower of St. Frideswide, in which those of Oxford had taken refuge, was burnt with them to the ground." This account is touched up by Mr. Andrew Lang with a little local colour :—"We are tempted to think of a low grey twilight above that wet land suddenly lit up with fire ; of the tall towers of St. Frideswyde's Minster flaring like a torch across the night ; of poplars waving in the same wind that drives the vapour and smoke of the holy place down on the Danes who have taken refuge there, and there stand at bay against the English and the people of the town." A finishing touch comes from the old chronicler, William of Malmesbury :—"Into the tower of St. Frideswyde they were driven, and as men could not drive them thence, the tower was fired, and they perished in the burning."

This closes the first era in the history of the church : the old *ecclesiola* of Didan and his daughter was gutted by the fire, and its roofs and furniture destroyed. Indeed, until lately it was held that the whole building was of wood, and perished therefore with the tower and roof, no vestige of it remaining for later times. But the recent investigations of Mr. J. Park Harrison, an archæologist of remarkable devotion and insight, have proved that the east wall of the eighth century church, with two of its primitive arches, still remains, a venerable relic of times past, as part of the wall of the cathedral; while the foundations of the three apses, into which the three low arches once led, have been discovered in the garden to the north-east of the church (see pp. 33, 34). So did Anthony a Wood, when in the seventeenth century he wrote of "the antientist buildings" as "on the east and north side of the church," speak more truth than even he himself was aware.

After the slaughter of St. Brice's Day, King Ethelred made a vow that he would rebuild St. Frideswide's church. And well did he keep it ; for in 1004 he built the splendid church which forms the main part of the cathedral as we know it to-day, sparing the more sacred part of the rude old building, it may be, because of the veneration in which everything connected with St. Frideswide was held. His charter contains the following sentence :—

"In the year of our Lord 1004, in the 2nd indiction, and in the 25th year of my reign, according to the disposal of God's providence, I Ethelred ruling over the whole of Albion, have with liberty of charters by royal authority and for the love of the Almighty, established a certain monastery situated in the city which is called Oxoneford, where the body of St. Frideswide reposes."

And here another question of the deepest architectural interest occurs. This church of Ethelred's was of a size and magnificence until lately considered not to have been attainable in England till many years after the Conquest. It was therefore taken for granted that the church was wholly rebuilt in the years 1160–1180, and that Ethelred's work was as entirely lost as Didan's was supposed to be. Dr. James Ingram, President of Trinity, had, it is true, written in the thirties to prove that the cathedral was Saxon, but, great authority as he was, he wrote at a time when architectural history was in its infancy; and at the restoration of 1869, Sir Gilbert Scott was content to write—"Dr. Ingram evinces great anxiety to prove that traces of his (Ethelred's) work still exist, but I need hardly say there is not a shadow of foundation for such a supposition." However, a greater authority than either of the preceding showed that the tide of knowledge was turning against the accepted view. Professor Freeman in his "History of Architecture" wrote that the cathedral might be "in the main portions of the fabric a monument of the later days of Saxon architecture," and that "the evidence between the conflicting statements which would assign it, some to the days of Æthelred II., others to those of Henry I., seems very evenly balanced;" in the former case, he said, "we have a complete minster of comparatively small size, but of the fullest cathedral type, belonging to the early part of the eleventh century." Mr. J. H. Parker, himself, who had been the chief authority for the theory that the Saxon architects built almost entirely in wood, at length changed his mind; and even went so far as to say, in the fourth edition of his "A. B. C. of Gothic Architecture," that "the Saxons, at the date of the conquest, appear to have been more advanced in the fine arts, such as sculpture, than the Normans," that "their work was more highly finished, had more ornament," and that their masonry was more finely jointed than that of the Normans.

Following up these admissions, Mr. Park Harrison carried on the most thorough investigations, examining almost every stone in the building, investigating Saxon MSS., and travelling over England and Normandy for the purposes of comparison. As a result he succeeded in convincing Professor Freeman, Professor Westwood, and other experts in Anglo-Saxon archæology, that Ethelred's church was still in the main extant; and at this moment his theory is very generally accepted. Without committing ourselves irrevocably to all Mr. Park Harrison's conclusions, some of which are naturally not so well established as others, we may, in the majority of cases, accept them, at least provisionally. Many allusions to them will occur in this book; and here, therefore, it is well to say that, while we think there is little likelihood of the whole theory being destroyed, we cannot venture to predict how much of it may be damaged or maintained by future research.

In this place the following summary of the evidence will suffice:—

1. There is no document or anything tending to show that the original fabric, as restored and enlarged by Ethelred, was ever rebuilt on a new plan.

2. Several of the choir capitals differ essentially in their ornamentation from any others in the cathedral; but resemble very closely the ornamental work in illuminated MSS. of Ethelred's time. They should consequently belong to the church as enlarged by him in 1004 (p. 72).

3. The junction of the eleventh century, or Ethelred's work with the later work, is clearly visible at the north and southwest corners of the choir; and the abaci, though resembling each other, are of different thickness. The ashlar work is different, and the courses are not continuous (p. 61).

4. The manner in which the Norman vaulting shafts are inserted in the north choir aisle implies that vaulting was not contemplated in the original plan of the church, and that the aisle was built at a date when vaulting ribs were not in use (p. 33).

5. The introduction of attached shafts in the tower piers shows that additions were made, about 1160, to earlier work with roll mouldings corresponding with those of the choir:

similar proofs of alteration are to be seen in the imposts of the tower and transept arches, which have been cut through to admit late Norman capitals (p. 58).

6. There is also good evidence that the Norman Presbytery is not part of the original choir, or the earliest part of the church, as was assumed, but probably stands on the site of an apse which belonged to Ethelred's building (p. 79).

7. The worn condition of the choir capitals can only be

CHRIST CHURCH FROM THE CANON'S GARDEN, 1857.

accounted for by the state of disrepair into which the church had fallen by the middle of the twelfth century (p. 74).

The reason is not far to seek for the unusual magnificence of Ethelred's plans. His brother-in-law was Richard II., Duke of Normandy, whose fame as an art-patron and church-builder was spread so far that, according to the Chronicles of

CHRIST CHURCH IN THE EIGHTEENTH CENTURY,

Fontenelle, " bishops and clergy, abbots and monks," travelled from all parts, from Greece and Armenia, to visit him, and William of Jumièges speaks of him as producing a kind of renaissance in his country. It so happens that one bay remains in the abbey church of Fécamp of the original building commenced by Duke Richard in 1001, just before Ethelred began his operations; and the capitals in this bay are ornamented with the same curious twining foliage that is found in the choir at Oxford. It is more than likely, then, that the Saxon king sought assistance from the cultured court of Richard-le-bon; the Queen Emma may well have been anxious to have the church rebuilt on a scale that would accord with the monastic buildings of her own land ; and so important was the work considered, that King Ethelred (as we learn from his charter) had contributions given him for carrying it on by his whole people.

But more troubles were to follow, for Ethelred had yet to pay the penalty for the massacre of St. Brice's Day, and his "long reign of utter misgovernment" was interrupted in 1013, when the heathen Viking Sweyn drove him out of his kingdom to take refuge in Richard's court in Normandy. The exile of the king, and the triumph of the Danes, who besieged and took Oxford in the same year, must have interrupted the work there for a time ; and a remarkable break of joint between the masonry of the choir and the south transept bears silent witness to the dislocation of the Anglo-Saxon rule (p. 61). When Sweyn died in 1014, Ethelred returned, and for three years, with the help of his noble son Edmund Ironside, héld Canute in check. At this time the work at St. Frideswide's was probably resumed, the king being doubtless anxious to complete the fulfilment of his vow at a time when he sorely needed the divine assistance ; and a certain difference in the character of the capitals and foliage in the transepts points to their having been built at this time, for they bear traces of oriental influence similar to that in the church at Bernay which Duke Richard was building in the year when Ethelred was with him in exile, and the eastern monks were flocking to his court in Normandy. But it is probable that, what with the strain of the terrible war, and the constant drain of the Danegelt, the work was never finished according to Ethelred's complete design, for he died in 1016, and his son Edmund Ironside only reigned for seven months.

Nor have we any record that anything further was done under Canute or Edward the Confessor. Though it is not at all improbable that Canute continued the work, for we know that he restored many monasteries which had been injured or destroyed by his father, being very fond of the monks; and that the Witenagemot met several times at Oxford during his reign. His marriage to Ethelred's widow Emma, also, placed him in the same relationship to the Norman court as Ethelred himself. The church must have been in use during this time; for we read that in the reign of Edward the Confessor troubles arose owing to the substitution of Regulars for the Secular Canons. Under King Harold the Seculars were restored, and, says Anthony Wood, "It was not long after this but that, whether by the negligence of the Seculars or the continuall disturbance of the expelled Regulars, it was almost utterly forsaken and relinqueshed, and the more especially because of that troublesome warre betweene King Harold and William the Conqueror,—a few persons all that while only remaining in it." In this ruinous state it proved a kind of white elephant that no one cared to possess; given first to Abingdon Abbey, and then to Roger, Bishop of Salisbury, it was at last handed over to Henry I., who made Guimond his chaplain Prior.

Although the whole church has been sometimes attributed to Prior Guimond, it is probable that he was too much taken up with restoring order to devote himself to architecture. And, as there is no suggestion in history that Ethelred's church was destroyed, so there is no mention of any building by Guimond. William of Malmesbury, his contemporary, praises his piety and learning (*excellentis literaturæ et non aspernandæ religionis*), but is totally silent about architectural talents. Besides, the establishment was at that time too impoverished for anything of the kind, many of the lands and revenues having been alienated, as we learn from the Domesday Book. If Guimond built at all, he would have had enough to do, we may imagine, in adapting the tumble-down monastic buildings for their occupation by canons regular. Sir G. G. Scott attributes the Norman doorway into the chapter-house to him; and he may have begun the restoration by putting a roof on the old church; for the weathered condition of some of the choir capitals bears out the historians who tell us that in the eleventh century the place was become ruinous.

Robert of Cricklade, called Canutus, another excellent man, was next prior. He ruled from 1141 to 1180. There was a copy of one of his works, says Dr. Ingram, in the library of Balliol College in Leland's time. In 1158 Cricklade obtained a confirmation of the privileges of the priory from Pope Hadrian IV. (Nicholas Brakespear, the English pope) who wore the tiara from 1154 to 1159. It was probably at this time that the restoration of Ethelred's church was begun, for the monks would almost certainly not have undertaken such extensive works until their property was secured them.

Robert of Cricklade did not build a new church, but it was probably he who restored Ethelred's church on the old plan, rebuilding those portions of the walls that required it, and inserting most of the later Norman work, especially the clerestory and presbytery. Much of the earlier work appears to have been imitated at this time, as is known to have been the case elsewhere when enlarging or rebuilding a church ; and some of the carved work was used again. Cricklade appears, from architectural evidence, to have left most of the old pillars, but he rebuilt two of those in the nave, and reduced the girth of the rest.

The restoration must have been pretty well finished by 1180, for in that year the relics of St. Frideswide were translated "from an obscure to a more noted place in the church," by the new prior Phillip, who himself wrote a book, " *De Miraculis S. Frideswydæ.*" The " obscure " place was doubtless the southernmost of the three early Saxon apses, recently discovered outside the east wall of the north choir aisle (see p. 37). So important a ceremony could not have taken place till the church was fit for the great company that assembled there ; for the translation was regarded as an event of national interest,—King Henry II. possibly, and the Archbishop of Canterbury certainly, being present, with many other prelates and nobles. This occasion may have also been the inauguration of Oxford University, since seven years afterwards we come upon the first mention of regular students.

Here is Wood's account of this the first translation :—

" After they were meet, and injoyned fasting and prayers were past, as also those ceremonies that are used at such times was with all decency performed, then those bishops that were appointed, accompanied with Alexio, the pope's legat for

Scotland, went to the place where she was buried, and opening the sepulchre, took out with great devotion the remainder of her body that was left after it had rested there 480 yeares, and with all the sweet odours and spices imaginable to the great rejoycing of the multitude then present mingled them amongst her bones and laid them up in a rich gilt coffer made and consecrated for that purpose, and placed it on the north side of the quire, somewhat distant from the ground, and inclosed it with a partition from the sight hereafter of the vulgar."

The fame of her miracles spread over all England, and multitudes came to be healed, many of whom went away whole and rejoicing.

But the troubles of the Priory were not yet over. During the priorate of Phillip in 1190, a great fire broke out in Oxford, which destroyed a large part of the city. St. Frideswide's did not escape, and, though the church itself does not seem to have suffered materially, it is probable that the monastic buildings were much injured, the chapter-house and cloisters among them ; for the old Norman doorway has, through all the changes of seven centuries, borne the red marks of the fire, and bears them as unmistakably to-day.

This mishap did not mark an era in the architecture of the church ; for nothing can with certainty be pointed to as the work of the last decade of the twelfth century ; nor indeed do we find that any important work was undertaken till, well into the thirteenth century, the spire was added. The monks seem to have patched up the ruined chapter-house as best they could, for it was not till about the middle of the thirteenth century that the present beautiful room was built. About this time the second bay of what is now the Latin Chapel was also added.

It seems certain now that the Lady Chapel, though it was undoubtedly vaulted, and its pillars cut into Early English shafts, was not built for the first time at this period. Part of the wall between it and the Latin Chapel remains in all its primitive roughness, while there is no sign of a wall between it and the north choir aisle. Its east wall is even older, for it contains one of the eighth century arches already alluded to.

In 1289, Robert de Ewelme being prior, the relics of St. Frideswide were again translated. "The old coffer," says the Oseney Chronicle, "of St. Fritheswyda was translated, and placed in a new and more precious one in the same church, and

near the place where the old one had stood." Its marble base
has recently been discovered, and replaced in what seems to
have been its old position.   The beautiful northernmost chapel,
called the Latin Chapel, was added in the fourteenth century,
the single Early English bay being incorporated, and the north
wall of the Lady Chapel further opened out, for this purpose.
Some of the Norman windows were also altered to Decorated.
The Norman windows at the east end were replaced by a large
five-light window, which was spoilt in the seventeenth century,
and ultimately removed by Sir Gilbert Scott.   Decorated
windows of three lights were also placed at the east ends of the
choir aisles, and a four-light window in the Lady Chapel.
These all went in the seventeenth century, but the beautiful
window in St. Lucy's Chapel survived.   All the fourteenth
century work belongs to a rather late division of the Decorated
style.

Towards the end of the fifteenth century the Perpendicular
style began to spread over the church.   Besides the windows
of the nave and north transept aisles, the clerestory of the choir
was remodelled to carry the elaborate vaulting, which was probably also added in this century, and not by Wolsey as has
been supposed, though the work may have been completed in
his time.   The similarity of the vaulting to that of the Divinity
School in Oxford enables us to fix the date pretty accurately
at 1480.

Another characteristic feature of the church was made at
this time, to wit, the fine chantrey tomb, called the Watching
Chamber, but very probably the third and last "shrine" of the
patron saint.   The cloisters were also reconstructed, and, in
order to make room for their eastern side, the western aisle of
the south transept was destroyed.

We are able to fix the date of the great north window of the
north transept, and of the commencement of vaulting in its
northern bay, because they were paid for out of a bequest of a
monk, James Zouch, who died in 1503, and is buried under
the window.   One may conjecture that the whole of the church
would have been vaulted in a style similar to that of the choir,
if the dissolution of the priory had not come, and left this one
bay as a pathetic little protest against the sweeping reconstruc-
tions of Cardinal Wolsey.

Indeed Wolsey, who in 1524 created Christ Church as a

C

college, did nothing but harm to Christ Church as a church.
It used to be thought that he had thrown the vault over the
choir, and even that he had built the palpably early English
spire!—an idea which throws a curious light upon the
architectural knowledge of our grandfathers. But, alas for
his reputation, the only work connected with the church that
can with certainty be attributed to him is the destruction of one
half of the nave. For, in order to build the great quadrangle
now known as " Tom Quad," he demolished its three western
bays, and was apparently only prevented from carting away the
whole church by his sudden fall from the royal favour in 1529.
His scheme for " Cardinal College," as Christ Church was at
first called, was one of extreme magnificence ; and he began—
much to the amusement of Oxford—with the splendid kitchen,
still in daily use. Tom Quad gives one some idea of the
scale on which he formed his plans : it, however, has never been
properly finished, as it is too large and too much inhabited to
be fit to receive the cloister for which it was designed. The
real cloisters are of much more modest dimensions. Wolsey
destroyed one side of them in order to build the college Hall.

In justice, however, to Wolsey it must be stated that he
commenced to build a new chapel along the north side of Tom
Quad, which, judging by the foundations that some draining
operations in the canon's gardens have recently disclosed,
would have rivalled the chapel of King's College, Cambridge, in
size, and have been about 100 feet longer than the actual length
of the cathedral. To this the Aubrey MSS. (written about
1670) refer :—" Ye foundations of that famous begun-Chapel
or Cathedral of Cardinal Wolsey which went towards the blue
Boare in Oxford and pulled down by Dean Fell about 1671."
Aubrey also mentions that the height of the walls of this
chapel was seven feet at the time of Wolsey's disgrace. The
west end ran in a line with the front of the octagonal turrets
in St. Aldate's Street, and the walls reached nearly to Fell's
passage into Peckwater.

To the sixteenth century belong also the flat wooden roofs of
the nave and transepts, and perhaps the concealment of the
lantern story of the tower.

The Reformation, apart from the usual destruction of altars,
furniture, plate, and ornamental work generally, is chiefly
remembered in the history of the church by the demolition of

St. Frideswide's shrine. Anthony a Wood says of the third shrine that, "being adored till the dissolution of the religious houses, it was then, 30 Henry VIII. [A.D. 1538], amongst others, taken down, and all the offerings conveyed into the King's Treasury." We give an account of the curious incidents connected with the demolition in our description of the shrine itself.

An inventory taken in the last year of Henry VIII.'s reign is interesting for the glimpse it gives us of the rich ornaments which even then survived, and must have made so vast a difference in the appearance of the church. They were confiscated, no doubt, as being "monuments tending to idolatrie and popish or devill's service, crosses, censars, and such lyke fylthie stuffe," to quote the curious phrases used by Bishop Horne of the plate of Trinity College.

There were eight altars in the aisles and body of the church, in addition to the high altar. The furniture then remaining of the high altar and choir was catalogued (only that the spelling was obscurer) as follows :—"Upon the high altar a here-cloth, 40s. *Item*, two altar-cloths, one of olde diaper, and the other of fine linen cloth. *Item*, a mass-book and a desk. *Item*, a great sacring bell. *Item*, 4 high latten candlesticks. *Item*, a canopy with a pix of copper. *Item*, 4 desks with two cloths of old silk. *Item*, a pair of organs, with a turned chain to the same. *Item*, 2 forms. *Item*, a canopy over the Dean's head of old silk. *Item*, 15 antiphoners and 9 grayells." After some more books comes :—"*Item*, a foot-cloth for the high altar of old tapestry." All the hangings of the side altars are enumerated, besides their vestments, candlesticks, etc. Thus the south choir aisle had " 4 hangings for above and beneath the altar, whereof two of white satin Bruges, and the other two of yellow and red," and two altar-cloths ; St. Lucy's Chapel had "two altar-cloths of old diaper, two hangings for the altar for above and beneath, the one of old needle-work, and the other of buckram " ; the four altars on the north of the choir were hung with "dornaxe," diaper, yellow and white baundkin.

The description of some. of the fourteen copes sounds very beautiful, for instance :—" 2 copes of red silk, woven with sunbeams of gold ; " "one cope of blue silk, woven with flower de luce, roses, and crowns of gold, and a whole suit to the same." There were also copes of purple and red, branched with gold, of red and white flowers, bordered with clouds, of red and green, of velvet and baundkin, and chamlet ; and many suits of vestments besides; and tunicles, albs, and amices for the choristers.

The inventory also contains, among other items, heavy silver bowls and other vessels belonging to the "house plate," and the "church plate," which we here give in the original spelling : —"A pixe of the ymage of God, gilte, weing 33 oz. *It^m·* a highe standing pixe wth a cover gilte, weing 23 oz. dim. *It^m·* a crosse wth Mary and John and a fote to the same gilte, weing 114 oz. *It^m·* a ship [incense-boat] and a spone gilte, weing 12 oz. dim. *It^m·* two bassings parcell gilte, weing 92 oz. *It^m·* a halliwater [holy water] bokett, and a sprinkell, whitt syluer, weing 33 oz., 2 greatt sensors, and a litle sensor, whit syluer, weing 170 oz. *It^m·* two crowetts [cruets] of whit syluer, weing 8 oz. *It^m·* a little paxe gilte, weing 3 oz. ; 4 chalesses, gilte, wth patentts, weing 95 oz. *It^m·* 3 chalesses wth patentt, whit syluer, weing 50 oz. *It^m·* a litle cros, parcell gilte, weing 51 oz. *It^m·* a crismatory gilte, not weighted. *It^m·* 2 gospells, plated wth syluer of thonesyde [the one side], not weighted. *It^m·* two maces for the preuelege, plated wth syluer vppon yeron [iron], not weighted. *It^m·* two virge roddes, plated wth syluer vppon yeron, not weighted ; 4 rectors · staves, the haadds of syluer wherof two gilte, not weighted. *It^m·* two stavis for the crosse, plated with syluer, not weighted."

When, in 1546, St. Frideswide's became the cathedral church of the four year old diocese of Oxford, the momentous change in its character left no mark upon its architecture. The great alterations in the fabric and fittings had either happened already or were yet to come.

During the deanery of Brian Duppa in 1630, the unhappy church suffered a sweeping restoration, which well-nigh destroyed its ecclesiastical character altogether. As Dean Duppa was a cultured man himself, and wrote a life of Michael Angelo, his work was all the more disastrous,—a mere Philistine would have probably been content to let well alone. To begin with, he, "*being minded to adorn it*," says Wood, "did first take down all the old stalls in the choir, and in their places put up those that now are," those great ugly pews, that is, which Dean Liddell removed. Then, in laying down his new pavement, he removed many of the old monuments, "having most of them," continues the old antiquary, "Saxon inscriptions on them ; which being looked upon by the dean and canons as old super-fluous stuff, and unhandsome to be mixed with their new pave-ment, they did cause them to be thrown out of the church, as also those out of the cloister." The remaining monuments he moved to the aisles, having, with two exceptions, "duly deprived them of their brasses." Thus was a priceless record of the priory's history lost to us. Most of his work has during this century been undone ; but one memorial of him remains, a valuable historical landmark, and full of the characteristics of its age—the Jonah window at the west of the north aisle of the nave.

In order that the windows of the aisles might be "beautified with glass, admirably well performed by the exquisite hand of Abraham Ling, a Dutchman, an. 1634," Brian Duppa and his chapter altered the whilom Perpendicular windows, sawing away "the fine architecture or crustation of those windows," and changing them from three lights with tracery to two plain lights, the author of the "Anatomy of Melancholy" being the donor of part of the new glass. The priceless old glass, which had been set up by ancient priors of St. Frideswide's, and con-tained pictures of the life of "The Lady," besides the arms of many benefactors, was ruthlessly sacrificed. This act of vandalism has led to still more unfortunate reprisals in our own time ; for Van Ling's old glass, which had great merits, was taken away at the last restoration, and replaced by some entirely uninteresting modern stuff (to say the least of it), while the tracery was remade into a respectable nineteenth century parody of the original Perpendicular.

The amiable and terrible Duppa also ruined the Decorated windows of three lights which terminated the aisles of the choir by converting them into his favourite two-light windows ; and the beautiful four-light window of the Lady Chapel was simi-larly treated. The great north transept window was likewise impoverished in its tracery ; and at the end of the seventeenth century the great east window was reduced from five to three lights by the same curious and unaccountable perversion of taste. One more memorial of Dean Duppa defaced the cathedral down to our time. This was the strange arrangement of stone screens by which the eastern chapels were separated from the transepts, and the most romantic feature of the church destroyed. They were particularly offensive, as they finished in a half-circle turned upwards, so that, with the Norman arch above, a complete circle was formed. However, the fine pulpit and organ-screen must be set down to the credit of this period.

Dean Duppa's successors signalised themselves, as far as the cathedral is concerned, only by the erection of monuments, some gruesome, and all heavy. Their work for the college was more considerable, and we shall enumerate it in our chapter on the Exterior.

A great deal of mischief was done to the painted glass during the Civil War, many of the windows being destroyed, and not one left quite perfect ; but otherwise the church escaped pretty well. Indeed, in this orderly country a great deal more damage has been done by lawful authority than by popular riots.

Up till Dean Liddell's time the cathedral was in as bad a state as most of the other cathedrals of England. A writer in the " Ecclesiologist " for February 1847 thus bewails its then condition :—

"We now come to the present estate of the cathedral, which is more deplorable than can be imagined. It is really wonderful that the cathedral of an English diocese, and the chapel of one of our greatest colleges, should remain in a condition which would disgrace the meanest hamlet. In the first place, it will hardly be credited by those whose eyes have not witnessed the sacrilege, that a portion of the church is actually desecrated. In so vast a college the hire of a single room cannot be dispensed with, but the House of God must be defiled ; a bay of the south transept and one of the adjoining chapels are blocked off to form a residence for the verger. On this subject we can hardly trust ourselves to speak.

"The fittings up of the choir are of the most wretched and irreverent description. The stalls are of seventeenth century work, and by no means a favourable specimen : those of the dean and canons are marked by canopies. The episcopal throne is meanness itself, and can hardly be distinguished without a most diligent search : on the prayer-books nearest to it, and nowhere else, are inscribed the words ' Christ-church Chapel,' as if to warn the Bishop off the forbidden ground. Nearly the whole area of the choir between the stalls is filled with benches looking west, and in which kneeling is all but impossible. These are occupied by the overgrown mass of undergraduates, and at the 'canons' prayers' partly by choristers. Further, that not an inch of available space may be lost, an arch on each side is blocked up by a gallery, which at surplice-prayers, when the students and commoners attend, is filled by the choir thus displaced. Finally, behind the stalls are some darksome dens, occupied by women, which greatly encumber the choir aisles. The screen [then blocking up the choir] is a cumbrous piece of work contemporary with the stalls, but of better character: it supports, of course, a vast and unsightly organ. The miserable appearance which is thus produced in this really noble chancel is almost indescribable. The whole seems so narrowed and confined ; one feels pent in without the least scope for one's energies. Of the service performed within the degraded choir we can only trust ourselves to say that it is the most slovenly and irreverent that we have ever witnessed in any English cathedral."

The stalls seem to have been particularly bad. The " Gentleman's Magazine " for 1856 says that " the choir aisles and the chapels were also excluded from view, and almost from any participation in the service, by the box-like framing, which rose to the height of eleven feet from the paving." Of course, all this had caused serious damage to the architecture : the pillars on the north and south side of the choir were, for instance, *squared*, and their bases cut away ; thus mutilated they had been "encased with heavily moulded Italian framing intermixed with some remnants of Jacobean workmanship."

But since the fifties the appearance of the cathedral has been completely changed. Dean Liddell began the restoration in 1856, when Mr. John Billing was employed to repair some parts of the walls that had become unsafe, and to remove the galleries and high pews. The work then done was only temporary ; the reseating whereby decent accommodation was provided for the whole college was managed out of the old woodwork, not a plank being taken out or carried into the church ; the organ was moved for the time into the south transept, so that the choir could be thrown open to the nave, and other work of a simple and necessary character carried through.

In 1870, Dean Liddell employed Sir G. Gilbert Scott to carry on the great restoration, whereby very considerable changes were wrought in the fabric itself.

On the whole, it has been real restoration, and not destruction : here and there one might have wished that the changes had been less sweeping, or that the renewed carved work had been left unattempted till such time as the dignity of labour in craftsmanship is recovered ; but it remains one of the most judicious and successful works of restoration that this not impeccable age has produced. The difficulties to be encountered were very great, for the church had suffered unusually ; a certain amount of rebuilding was therefore inevitable, and besides provision had to be made for the church as a college-chapel as well as a cathedral.

The restoration was preceded by a report on the condition of the building, which Sir Gilbert Scott drew up in 1869. The following extract shows the " reparation " that was needed :—

" It is fortunately the case that the main walls of the building do not show any symptoms of failure or of weakness. The external stone-work is very unequal in its state of preservation, some parts being very much decayed, while others have suffered in a very small degree. On the whole, however, there can be no doubt that the decay is very extensive, and even some parts which, at first sight, seem tolerably sound, are found on closer examination to be seriously decayed. The eastern parts are, as a rule, better preserved than those facing in other directions, though the southern aisle of the choir is also among the least decayed portions. The tower is generally very severely decayed, but the spire less so, though its lights are very much damaged. The reparation of this wide-spread decay is a work requiring much discrimination and judgment. Every stone which retains ancient work in an intelligible state should be carefully preserved, and only such parts renewed as have become shapeless from decay, or the retention of which would tend to future injury.

" Internally, the stone-work generally needs little more than the careful brushing or washing off of the white-wash and the exposure of the original surfaces. This should be effected with extreme care and tenderness, so as not to efface in any degree the original tool-marks or to disturb any ancient wall-painting which may exist. The mutilations which the work has in some places suffered would of course be repaired, as well as any structural defects which may be brought to light."

This proves that Gilbert Scott went to work with a full

sense of his responsibility, so far as the "reparation" was concerned. With regard to the "restoration," many compli-cated questions arose, but Scott generally threw his weight on the conservative side, respecting all the alterations which had been effected before "the extinction of our national architecture in the sixteenth century"; and, happily, respecting as well all the good work of a later date. Thus the organ-case and pulpit were spared. Duppa's work was mostly destroyed, his windows being rebuilt according to their former Perpendicular and Decorated designs, with the one interesting exception already mentioned. To make provision for the church's collegiate use, while rendering it at the same time suitable for diocesan purposes, an iron screen was carried round the nave as well as the choir, and the seats of the nave were set lengthways. This arrange-ment could not well have been bettered : the college is well accommodated without any blocking up of the church, and the choir is conveniently situated in the eastern bay of the nave. The organ at the same time was moved to the west end of the church, where a new bay was made ; and thus, while an increased effect of length was given, a screen was provided for the college-chapel, without hiding any of the old work in the nave, and the choir was no longer hidden by the organ.

The great Decorated east window, which had been spoilt in the seventeenth century, was, after much deliberation, removed ; and, traces being found of a large circular window assumed to be Late Norman, the east end was rebuilt in accordance with the conjectured Norman design,—a bold venture, but a remark-ably successful one. At the same time the two Norman windows at the sides of the presbytery were reopened.

The bay of the south transept, which had been cut off, and used as a house for the verger, was recovered, and the present vestry built therein, in a style, right no doubt in general plan, but not very successful in detail.

The vaulting of the cloister was completed, and, by the happy expedient of building a raised wooden vault in one part, the old chapter-house door was once more fully exposed to view. The division which had entirely spoilt the chapter-house itself was removed ; as were also the stone screens which had cut off and defaced the beautiful cluster of north-eastern chapels.

The opening of the lantern-story added greatly to the beauty of the interior, but it made it necessary to chime the bells

instead of ringing them ; and in 1878 they were removed altogether, as their vibration was considered dangerous to the
tower, and an admirably contrived belfry built in 1880 over the
staircase of the Hall by Mr Bodley. This architect also constructed the porch which opens into Tom Quad, and affords
an entrance to the cathedral at once more dignified and convenient than before.

Since Scott's time a good many further improvements have
been effected, among which may be mentioned the reredos, the
stained glass of Sir Edward Burne Jones, the fitting up of the
Latin Chapel and recovery of the easter sepulchre therein, the
recovery also of the marble base of the second shrine of St.
Frideswide, and of the early Saxon arches hard by.

At least it cannot be true now, as it seems to have been fifty
years ago, that many persons, visiting Oxford to explore its
antiquities, " actually go away without entering the cathedral
church, or that undergraduates any longer pass an academical
career, content to be aware possibly that Christ Church has
its chapel, like other colleges."

CHAPTER II.

THE peculiar position of Christ Church, as a cathedral which is three parts college chapel, is apparent to the most casual observer, who, passing by the college porter in the gateway of Tom Tower, finds himself in a great open quadrangle with a fine hall on one side, but no sign of a cathedral anywhere, except a spire which seems so far off that it might very well belong to some other college. He may well be struck by that doubtfulness as to any means of exit, which makes most of the colleges appear to the stranger as if they consisted of one quadrangle only. There really seems no way of getting to the cathedral, for the incipient cloisters of Tom Quad stretch in unbroken array round the four points of the compass ; and no one could be expected to guess that the two rat-holes at one side of the eastern terrace stand for the west front of a great church. But so it is, and on Sundays a crowd of citizens mingle with the undergraduates in their curious open surplices, and drift across the Quad, past Mercury fountain, leaving no doubt in the mind of the traveller that this is a cathedral church, and he is as free of it as anybody else. There is, indeed, another entrance from the old cloister on the south side, which is public, though mainly convenient to those members of "The House" who dwell in the Old Library and Meadow Buildings ; and a third entrance besides, which is, however, the private boon of the Professor of Pastoral Theology.

It follows, therefore, that without describing the various college buildings, which are rather outside our province, we can say little about the exterior, except in matters of detail ; for there is no close, and the cathedral is thus far from being common property that it is hidden in a rather intricate environ-

ment of college buildings and private gardens. But the one
feature which in part rises above its misfortunes is the spire.

The Spire.—Among all the strange domes and steeples
which give to the city of Oxford such a unique appearance,
this spire of the cathedral is to the architectural eye not the
least striking. Very humble in its bearing, it seems to put
forward no claim to our attention, and may escape the notice
of a hurried traveller; but it has more character and interest
than the elaborate spire of the University Church itself. Its
very modesty gives it a distinction; were it taller it would be
but one among a hundred, but as it is there is no other in
England at all like it in the quiet dignity of its low proportions.
The first time one sees it one is most struck by its squat
appearance; it seems almost to have been built as little more
than a convenient stone capping for the tower; and, indeed,
each time one returns to Oxford one is struck afresh by this
lowliness; so that one fancies for a moment that it may have
subsided a little during one's absence. But it quickly resumes
its old dignity—the kind of dignity that one sometimes notices
in short people—and every day it seems to grow a little higher.
Homely and simple, as befits the crown of a foundation which
is called "The House," it wins an almost human place in the
affections of those who live near it; and never was a spell so
honestly cast, never a friend that bore so well the test of
familiarity.

And its low proportions are soon accounted for. It is one
of the earliest spires (perhaps the very first) ever built in
England. Thus it was an experiment in what must have
appeared at the time a very hazardous style of building; and
that which to us is low, to the men of the thirteenth century
must have seemed dangerously lofty. It was a pioneer, and as
such needed to be sturdy. We need not then regret that it is
not like that of Salisbury; it gives the whole cluster of buildings
a look of security, and it causes no anxiety to its guardians.

"This spire," wrote Dr. Ingram in 1837, "certainly accords
in character with some of the earliest specimens in Oxfordshire
and Northamptonshire, measuring in height about two diameters
of its base; and it is remarkable, that the small turrets at the
angles of the north transept are made to terminate in pyramidal
octagons, similar to those which surmount the angles of the
tower. These are the simple prototypes of those exuberant

THE TOWER AND SPIRE, FROM THE CLOISTERS.

pinnacles, niches, and tabernacles, enriched with crockets and finials, which so profusely embellish the spires and turrets of a later date. A singular specimen of this improved kind of turret is seen on the north side of the cathedral; beneath which is an elegant niche, containing a statue of St. Frideswide."

The lower story of the tower is Norman, or earlier, with later work added. The belfry-stage and the spire are early English. On each side of the lower story can be seen the line of the ancient high roof, destroyed in the Perpendicular period, to the great loss of the exterior effect, which Sir Gilbert Scott was anxious to restore. On either side of the roof-line is a plain window. At each angle a circular turret supports the tower, the turret being reduced in size at the belfry-stage where the Early English work commences, and ornamented with a tall and graceful arcade; an arcade being also carried all round the walls of the belfry-stage, and its central arches pierced for windows. Each turret finishes above the belfry-stage in a pinnacle. "These pinnacles," says Mr. R. J. King, "are modern; but are faithful, or, more truly, servile imitations of the ancient ones; of which not only the original features, but those resulting from the wear and tear of six centuries, have been too exactly copied."

The spire itself is octagonal, with circular ribs at the angles; it is of the " broche " form, that is to say, it rises from the exterior of the tower walls, like most others of that period. Its eaves are supported by a corbel-table of pointed arches; and from its cardinal faces project the four spire lights of the same graceful character as the arcading of the belfry-stage. When the upper part of the spire was restored, the beautiful finial of foliage was for some unaccountable reason not reproduced. The old spire point was erected in one of the canon's gardens, where it rests in peace.

The tower can best be seen from the cloister, the staircase window in the Library in Peckwater Quad, and the canon's garden on the north side. Of course, there are many distant points of view; but one from the path between the Broad Walk and Merton College gives a better idea of the cathedral as a whole than most.

The tower can be ascended from the gallery in the south transept, but it should not be attempted by any but slim persons. The visitor makes his way along the clerestory and round the lantern, which is the first stage of the tower. Having avoided the iron bars which threaten him at every turn, he will have to squeeze through an incredibly small doorway, and then climb up a dark staircase which takes him, not into the belfry, but into the spire. One can only peer into the lower part of the belfry from the shuttered windows on the outside ; but as the interior of the spire is open to it, the whole, forming one queer-shaped room, can be seen therefrom. The bells have all gone, as they taxed the strength of the tower, having been originally cast for the larger tower of Oseney Abbey (see p. 43) ; they are now hung in the new bell-tower over the hall staircase. The belfry-stage can be considered octagonal from the interior, four very short extra sides being formed by the angular turrets, which are chamfered off on the inside. Above these are the squinches which support the spire. Round the arcade which contains the belfry windows runs a passage, made just like the clerestory passage of a church. The whole structure is re-markable for its careful and finished work, the very corbels just above the floor being heavily foliated, as if they were intended to be seen from below.

The windows of the spire are interesting for the double plane of tracery which adds to the strength of the spire. The inner tracery resembles that without, with the difference that it has no transom. The transom, by the way, is a rare feature in the Early English period.

The only exterior view of any extent is from the garden of the Professor of Pastoral Theology on the northern side of the cathedral. It seems unfortunate that so important a spot should be in private hands, and the public excluded ; but still a visitor who desires to go into the garden can obtain per-mission by applying at the professor's house in Tom Quad. The garden is a pretty one, and the view of the homely-looking cathedral set in this quiet old-fashioned retreat is well worth taking the trouble to see. The Latin Chapel, which seems to stand right on the lawn, looks like some little village church, while the north transept seems inconceivably smaller than from the inside.

From between the transept and the nave, near the house that is to say, there is an excellent view of the tower.

Two remarkable square turrets flank the transept : they re-semble those at the east end, and are nearly of the same date ;

they are, however, capped by pinnacles like those on the tower, but somewhat earlier. At the angle of the transept aisle there is a smaller turret, early Perpendicular in style, with crockets on its spire, and in its west face a niche with a weather-worn statue of St. Frideswide. The flowing tracery of the four beautiful windows of the Latin Chapel is well seen from here ; and the buttresses that support its wall should also be noticed.

The Saxon Apses.—In this garden can also be seen the site of the Saxon apses, discovered in 1887 by Mr. Park Harrison. The history of this discovery is an extremely interesting one. It was known that two small rag-stone arches existed at the east end of the Lady Chapel and

EARLY SAXON ARCHES.

north choir aisle, though blocked up and concealed by plastering inside the church. Their character and rude workmanship suggested that they formed part of the original church of the Holy Trinity, St. Mary, and All Saints, which was built c. 727 ; but there was some years ago a tradition among architects that nearly all Saxon churches were built of wood, and the presumption naturally was that the original church was entirely destroyed in the fire of 1002. However, it came gradually to be admitted, even by the late Mr. J. H. Parker, that Saxon churches were built of stone from the earliest times ; it was further found to be implied by the charter of Ethelred that the old church had been of stone ; for the charter states that,

D

when it was found necessary to dislodge the Danes by burning, the fire was thrown upon the wooden shingles of the roof. Another document supported this theory by stating that Ethelred " repaired and enlarged " the old building. Thus the presumption lately came to be that these arches, and the wall in which they stood, belonged to the church of 727.

In opposition to this it was suggested that they were nothing more than barrow-holes made in the twelfth century to admit the Norman workmen. Mr. Harrison, however, was strongly opposed to this view, urging that no barrow-holes existed of such narrow dimensions as these doors, or in such an incon-

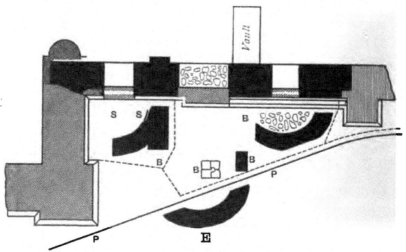

PLAN OF RECENTLY EXCAVATED SAXON ARCHES.[1]

venient place as the east wall of a chapel. In order to put his conviction to the test he asked that excavations should be made outside the east wall, to see if the doorways led into a crypt or " porticus," since apses, used for interments, had been found of an equally early date at Winchester and Lyminge.

This venture of faith was triumphantly rewarded by the discovery in 1887 of the foundations of three apses, corresponding with these two arches, and with a third between them, of which traces were found shortly after. The first excavation in

---

[1] s. *Skeletons* ; B. *Bones* ; P. *Drain-pipe.*

the canon's garden took the form of a trench outside the
southern arch, and led to the discovery of part of the foundation of an apse, which measured a quarter-circle. The rest
of this foundation had been destroyed, evidently when the
wall of the Norman presbytery was built (which, it is notable, is
quite twelve inches thicker than the wall containing the arches);

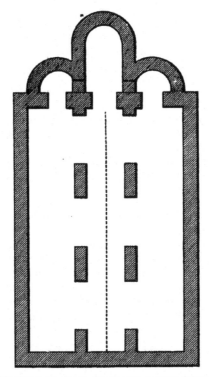

CONJECTURAL PLAN OF EARLY SAXON CHURCH.

but it was evident that the archway in the wall must have stood
in the centre of a perfect apse. Similar foundations were next
laid bare opposite the northern arch. Then the earth was removed opposite the Norman pilaster buttress, which, standing
midway between the two arches, led the investigators to suppose

that it hid a centre Saxon archway. Nothing was found at first
but a small piece of concrete walling (2 feet by 1½ feet) which
it was at once seen might prove to be part of the north wall of the
chancel of the ancient church, if a centre apse could be proved
to have projected beyond the two side apses. Excavations
were therefore commenced further east, with the result that
the foundations of the central apse were discovered under a
drive in the garden. The missing portion of this apse was
accounted for by a main drain which had been cut across
its inner side, and by a pit which had been made for the
interment of bones found elsewhere in the Close. About the
same time Mr. A. J. Evans, the Keeper of the Ashmolean
Museum, found rag-stones by the side of the Norman buttress,
which proved to be part of the central archway, a little wider
and higher than the two side ones. It now became clear that
this archway was really not a doorway at all but a small chancel-
arch, the three arches being similar to those still used in the
conservative churches of the East. It is a foot wider than the
chancel-arch of the Saxon church at Bradford, Wilts, and two feet
wider than the arch between the tower and chancel of Wotten
Wawen church in Warwickshire, the jambs and arches of which
were also built of rag-stone. Further evidence of the antiquity
of this east wall is the fact that the sill of the south archway
was found to be 2 feet 8 inches below the level of the pavement
of the Norman church, as is shown in the elevation.

This Eastern plan of three apses was adopted about the
same early period at Melbourne and Lindisfarn ; and, as it was
not long before the death of the great Archbishop Theodore
that this arrangement came in, there is a great probability that
he introduced it from his native country of Syria, where the
churches were always constructed with three apses. The
absence of any marks of juncture upon the exterior of the walls
also inclines one to suspect that there was a passage from apse
to apse behind the wall, as there always is in Eastern churches.
The whole arrangement will be made abundantly clear from
the above conjectural ground-plan of the ancient church, c. 740.

There are indications that these three apses are not of precisely the same date, for the northernmost arch is the smallest
of the three, and the apse is correspondingly smaller. It is
therefore surmised that the southernmost apse belonged to the
church of Didan, the father of St. Frideswide, and dedicated to

the Holy and Undivided Trinity, "without any more title and addition," while the other apses were the additions of Frideswide herself, when the church was adapted to the purposes of a convent, with the additional dedication to St. Mary and All Saints. This may be the reason why the chapel in a line with the central apse, and therefore on the site of the ancient nave, is still the Lady Chapel.

Another important point rests upon the document which states that, when Ethelred II. enlarged and repaired the old building, the result was that the tomb of St. Frideswide, which before was on the south side of the church, thereupon stood in the middle. The tomb of St. Frideswide must therefore have been in the southernmost of these three apses (in a "chapel," as Wood says, on the south side of the convent church), and not, as some people have supposed, in the vault discovered under the tower during Scott's restoration. A significant corroboration of the old document is supplied by the fact that the Norman plinth, which was carried across the other two archways, breaks off at the arch which leads into the south apse. It would thus seem that access was, after the Norman restoration, still afforded into this chapel, and that St. Frideswide's relics remained there until the Translation of 1180, when they were moved "from an obscure to a more noted place in the church" on the completion of the Norman ·restoration.

After the investigations had been completed, the earth was laid down again, but stones have been set in the drive to mark the site of the old foundations. Some charcoal and reddened stone which was found—evidently a relic of the fire of 1002— is now to be seen in the gallery over the vestry in the cathedral. In addition to this, the remains of a rough pavement were exposed in the north apse, and some square stones in the chord of the central apse, which seem to be part of the old altar. In addition to the numerous scattered bones that the workmen unearthed, two complete skeletons were found in the southern apse, and underneath the stone slabs upon which they lay another skeleton, that of a woman or a man of short stature, possibly that of Didan himself, or his wife Saffrida, who are both known to have been buried in the church.

The Cloister now forms only three sides of a square, the western part having been destroyed by Wolsey in order to make room for the hall staircase. Considerably inferior to those of Magdelen and New College, it is small and unpretentious : its tracery, of a humdrum Perpendicular type (mostly restored), and its vaulting, which is peculiar, point to the latter half of the fifteenth century as the time of its erection. Of the earlier cloister no trace remains, except the door and windows of the chapter-house. The north walk was converted into a muniment room, much to the defacement, one may imagine, of this part of the college; but it has now been restored, and a good imitation of the fine old lierne groined roof inserted, though funds have not been provided to finish the carving of the bosses. Mr. R. J. King points out that the panelling of the sides of the windows agrees very closely, even to the character of the cusps, with that introduced into the clerestory of the choir. The quadrangle of the cloister was the scene of Cranmer's degradation. In its area are the foundations of the lavatory, which was built about 1490.

Above the arches of the cloister runs a story with latticed windows on the east and south side, which adds considerably to the picturesqueness of the whole. Indeed, as one stands on the steps leading to the hall, the ivy-grown cloister, in spite of its modest proportions, has a beauty of its own. The latticed windows give it an air of mystery, as if strange old rooms were concealed by them; and in fact on the south side there is a curious library of time-worn theological books, which is seldom entered, and hardly ever used. The windows on the east side hide nothing more romantic than a small lumber-room, cut up by the raising of the wooden roof beneath, and an undergraduate's bed-chamber.

From the same position at the west of the cloister one can enjoy the best view of the tower and spire of the church. One is close enough to see all the detail, and yet from this angle nothing is lost of the general effect. On a moonlit evening the effect is particularly solemn and beautiful. From this point also should be noticed the difference in the masonry of the south transept. The lower story is entirely of rubble, while the upper story is partly of good ashlar work.

On the south side of the cloister is the Old Library, as it is now called, which was formerly the refectory of the monastery, and is all that now remains of the conventual buildings. Its large Perpendicular windows, rising like a clerestory above it, look on to the cloister, but they were spoilt on the inside by a staircase, when the building was turned into undergraduates' rooms. On the other side, facing the meadow buildings, there is a curious little oriel window, its lights now walled up, that once contained the pulpit whence the lessons were read during meals. The rest of the Perpendicular windows on this side are entirely gone, and the beauty of what was one of the best buildings in Oxford destroyed. An engraving of the Refectory in its original state is given in Skelton.

DOORWAY OF CHAPTER HOUSE.

The roof, which formerly hid the upper part of the chapter-house door, has been removed, and, by a happy device, a wooden roof groined in the same way has been inserted at a higher level, thus giving the old doorway the benefit of its full proportions. This doorway has been attributed to Prior Guimond, and belongs mainly to the later Norman period, of which it is a fine example. The two inner divisions of the arch are richly ornamented with zigzag moulding ; the two outer divisions rest on shafts, of which the pair on the north have sculptured, and the pair on the south plain cushion, capitals. On either side of the doorway is a round-headed window of two lights, plain without, but ornamented within with the same label as that which surrounds the outer arch of the doorway itself. An ancient painting can be made out on the north side of the northernmost of these windows ; it was traced recently, and found to be the figure of a saint.

The Chapter-House was rebuilt in the very best Early English period, of which it is an excellent example. It bears some resemblance to the chapter-house at Chester, being especially remarkable for the purity of its style and the excellence of its detail.   It would, indeed, be hard to find a better specimen of a mediæval chamber.

As the whole effect of the room depends upon its proportions, it is hardly necessary to say that the extraordinary genius for making the worst of everything, which seemed at one time to take possession of the English people, inspired some one to build a wall right across the middle.   This has, however, been removed, and the visitor has now nothing to complain of but a want of colour.   The chapter-house has been used for divinity lectures since the Latin Chapel was restored to its original purpose; and the lower part of the walls is now hung with curtains, which help to destroy the coldness due to the destruction of the old painting and furniture.

CORBEL IN CHAPTER-HOUSE.

The room is an oblong, divided into four bays, the vaulting of which springs from clustered shafts, supported on curiously carved corbels.   Two of these corbels are in the form of monks' heads, very vividly conceived; they face each other, and are thought, from the vivacity of their expression, to be represented as carrying on a conversation together.   The perfect taste of the rich carving on the bosses of the roof will also be noticed. One of them represents our Lady crowned, in the act of giving an apple to the Holy Child.

But the most striking feature of the chapter-house is its east end.   An arcade of five arches fills the entire space ; of these the three central arches are pierced for windows, deeply recessed, and having a double set of shafts to support their arches, the inner shafts being clustered, and ornamented with dog-tooth moulding.   Each light is crossed by a transom, with a later four-centred arch beneath.   Foliage is introduced in the spandrels, and every capital in the room is richly foliated, nor could anything exceed the grace and finish of the carving. There are two windows of similar character on the south side of the room, and one on the north.   There are also some pieces of remarkably fine glass in these side windows, which one should be careful not to miss. The remains of painting on the groined ceiling are not likely to escape notice,—the figures of St. Peter and St. Paul can be easily distinguished.

A thirteenth century stone slab now rests in the chapter-house; it was brought here from Rewly Abbey, where it covered the tomb of Ela, wife of Thomas de Newburgh, Earl of Warwick, and daughter of William Longspée. In the east wall is preserved the foundation stone of Wolsey's College at Ipswich, the inscription on which runs,—"*Anno Christi 1528, et regni Henrici octavi, regis Angliae 20, mensis vero Junii 15, positum per Johannem epm. Lidensem,*"—John Holt being titular Bishop of Lydda, and probably a suffragan of Lincoln. The stone has no connection with Christ Church, beyond the fact that it commemorates another

BOSS IN CHAPTER-HOUSE.

benefaction of Wolsey, and was presented to the House in 1789.

A small staircase in the south wall leads up into the charming oak-panelled room, which is used by the chapter for meetings. In the window of the staircase will be noticed some initial letters and other devices in stained glass which are among the very finest of their kind. In the upper room itself, which looks pleasantly on to a garden, are some interesting pictures:—one of Henry VII.; another of the same king, younger, with his queen; Henry VIII.; Elizabeth; Mary; Samuel Fell, the father of Bishop Fell, and Dean of Christ Church himself; Busby, the terrible headmaster of Westminster School, also connected with this House; two portraits of the talented Dean Aldrich, and one of Peter Martyr, whose wife was so strangely made to share the grave with St. Frideswide. Peter Martyr had been himself an Augustinian prior: he adopted strong reforming views, and was made Regius Professor of Divinity here in 1549. He lived near Tom Gate; but the undergraduates broke his windows, and he moved to the cloister, where he fortified his garden. According to Blunt, he gave up the professorship when the undergraduates annoyed him, but returned on being made a canon. In this chapter-room there is a good Elizabethan table, a curious old iron safe, and some Chippendale chairs.

A gateway in the cloister to the north of the chapter-house

THE CHOIR, FROM THE OLD CEMETERY.

leads into the slype, which occupies the position usual in monastic buildings between the chapter-house and the transept. In this case the slype is a plain barrel-vaulted passage that takes up part of the transept itself, and forms the lower story of the choir-vestry (as it now is) within the church. It leads into the old cemetery, whence a good view is obtained of St. Lucy's chapel, the east end, and the chapter-house. In the garden are the tombs of Philip Pusey, son of Dr. Pusey, and Edith Liddell, who is commemorated in St. Catherine's window. The round-headed doorway, now blocked up, should also be noticed: it may be one of the doorways of Ethelred's church, and is in any case the only ancient one left.

The east end was restored in 1871 by Gilbert Scott, in accordance with the late Norman design, of which fragments, left when the Decorated window was inserted, still remained in the wall ; but how far exactly it follows the original no one appears to know.

An elaborate wheel-window occupies the upper part of the chancel gable ; above it is a blind arcade of transitional pointed arches, and below are two round-headed windows. The square turrets at the angles are ornamented with arcading in three stories : the upper is on a level with the pointed arcading of the main wall, and similar in style ; the middle carries on the line of the wheel-window, and consists of two round arches on each turret ; the lower, on a level with the two round-headed windows, is made up of three round arches, which, by intersecting, form four pointed arches. The whole, in spite of its being (with the exception of the turrets) a restoration, gives one a good idea of transitional work on a large scale. In plan it is still Romanesque, in detail it is Early Gothic.

The Bell Tower, which stands above the hall-staircase, is really only a stone case built by Mr. Bodley to hide the wooden structure which actually contains the bells. The tower, as it now stands, is incomplete, Mr. Bodley having intended a lofty and intricate wooden superstructure to rest upon it. The authorities, however, were afraid of its dwarfing the spire and Tom Tower, and consequently left the structure in its present state, much against the opinion, as we understand, of the architect, whose completed design can be seen in the common-room, and is so magnificently picturesque, that one cannot help hoping that the authorities will see their way to erecting it. After all, if every one in the past had been afraid of overtopping the cathedral, Oxford would never have become the " Sweet city of her dreaming spires" that we know. The cathedral can hold its own, and so can Tom Tower ; for neither makes any pretensions to loftiness. The original hall-tower seems to have stood on the same spot before the space was cleared for the erection of Dean Fell's staircase.

The bells themselves are, with Great Tom, the only relics left of the glorious Abbey of Oseney. They were considered the finest in England, and were after their removal to the cathedral made famous again as "The merry Christ Church bells" of Dean Aldrich's catch. Their names are contained in the following line, which professes to be a hexameter—

Hautclerc, Douce, Clement, Austin, Marie, Gabriel et John.

TOM TOWER.

Tom Tower, over the entrance to Tom Quad from St. Aldate's, is one of the characteristic features of the city. The lower story was built by Wolsey, but the cupola which gives it so uncommon an appearance was added by Sir Christopher Wren in 1682. On the side facing St. Aldate's is a statue of the great Cardinal, in a very dramatic attitude, and on the quadrangle face a statue of Queen Anne, placed there by her minister Harley, with this inscription,—*Annae Principi Optimae Secretarius ipsius principalis Robertus Harley hac in sede posuit*

THE WESTERN ENTRANCE AND BELL TOWER, FROM TOM QUAD.

quod illam coleret et hanc amaret. The vault of the archway
under Tom Tower is decorated with the arms of those who
helped towards the completion of the quadrangle. "Tom," the
great bell which gives its name to the quadrangle, and its
orders to the whole University, came, with the cathedral bells,
from Oseney Abbey; and twenty shillings were paid in 1545
for the conveyance of Tom and his satellites from the Abbey
to Christ Church. It weighed 17,000 pounds, and bore the
inscription,—*In Thomae laude resono Bim Bom sine fraude ;* but
it was recast in 1680, and its present inscription is *Magnus
Thomas Clusius Oxoniensis renatus Apr. 8, 1680.* It will have
to be recast again some day, for it is sadly out of tune; its
note ought to be B flat, but is not, and the bell itself is
cracked.

Perhaps the other college buildings are sufficiently connected
with the history of the cathedral to allow of our mentioning
them. For Wolsey built the kitchen, which is a remarkably
fine specimen of the peculiar architecture necessitated for such
a building, and also the magnificent hall, the finest perhaps in
England, and interesting to us also as containing the portraits
of many of the men referred to in this book. Wolsey also
built three sides of Tom Quad. Though the bases of the
buttresses for its cloister invite the enterprising builder, the
Quad is probably best left as it is ; for a projecting cloister is
not anything the architectural success that a cloister is which
forms the ground story of a building continued over it, and the
Quad is besides so large as to be unmanageable in the matter
of cloisters. The fountain in the middle is called "Mercury,"
because Dr. Anthony Radcliffe set up a statue there of the
nimble god. Frank Buckland, by the way, about five years
before his death, put into Mercury several golden carp ; there
was also added an *Aurea Tinca* from Austria, a superb creature,
popularly called "The Dean." The surface of the Quad was in
1665 lowered three feet, so as to give a greater appearance of
height to the surrounding buildings. Bishop John Fell finished
the quadrangle, and his father, Dean Samuel Fell, built the
vaulted staircase of the Hall (1640), which is one of the instances
of the curious survival of Gothic in Oxford, that home of "lost
causes," which need never have been lost, and of "impossible
ideals," which ought to be made possible. Late as it is, and
open to the structural criticism of all Perpendicular work,

it is most deservedly admired. The staircase itself must not
be laid to Fell's charge; it is the work of the James Wyatt.
Dean Aldrich built Peckwater Quad, which is a decent work
of its kind, too grim and gloomy to be as attractive as All
Saints Church, and dreadfully disfigured by the strange ten-
dency to moulder away that besets Headington stone, from
which Oxford as a whole has suffered so much.

The Library in Peckwater Quad was begun in 1716 (designed
by Dr. G. Clerke), and finished in 1761, the original intention
having been to leave an open piazza beneath it; but its columns
were connected, in the end, by a wall. It contains a few first-
rate pictures (including an exquisite Francesca) among a great
many palpable shams, and a collection of drawings mainly by
fifteenth and sixteenth century artists, which are said to have
given Ruskin his first enthusiasm for Italian art, when he was
an undergraduate at the House. Wyatt was the architect of
Canterbury Gate.

Dean Liddell built the Meadow Buildings nearly thirty years
ago; the architect was Mr. T. Deane. They are as bad as the
other college buildings in Oxford of the same period.

CHAPTER III.

THE cathedral is best entered through the handsome porch in Tom Quad which was cut by Mr. Bodley through one of the canonical houses ; in order, perhaps, to announce that the old *régime* had passed away, and the time at last arrived when " the teachers of theology no longer dwell on the ruins of the church they should protect," as a writer fifty years back had half-despairingly foretold. This porch is a happy compromise between the old heart-breaking descent into a half-ruined nave, and the rather impossible scheme of continuing the church into the middle of the Quad. The former spoilt the cathedral, the latter would have spoilt the college ; but by the present arrangement the church serves very creditably for both its purposes, and one may well spend a day there without remembering what Wolsey did to the nave.

On entering the cathedral itself the visitor finds himself in a kind of narthex which is in fact the ante-chapel of a college chapel. Before him is the organ-screen, the entrance under which is veiled by a curtain at service time ; on either side he has a glimpse of the aisles. The effect is peculiar, but not unpleasant, although the ante-chapel is a bare bit of modern restoration, wisely left unsculptured, and unrelieved except for some monuments, of which one may gratefully say that they are best where they are. But passing under the screen, all is changed. We find ourselves in one of the most charming and distinctive interiors of a country of interesting churches. The curious and happy arrangement of the great pillars and triforium, the variety and originality of the sculptured capitals, the rich pendent vaulting of the choir, and the touch of mystery in the further chapels, all combine to give to this

E

creation of a long and chequered history an attraction peculiarly its own.

Yet the same bluntness of aspect which impresses one in the spire is the leading characteristic of the interior also. Only in this case the effect is not part of the original plan, but is due to the destruction by Wolsey of the three Western bays. Things must have seemed far worse before the new western bay added twenty feet to the nave, and brought the church right back to the cloister around Tom Quad, for though it only serves as an ante-chapel, it yet helps considerably to break the enclosed appearance, which must have been almost oppressive before.

As it is, Christ Church is the smallest of our cathedrals ; for even with the new ante-chapel it measures but 175 feet in length. Instead of being of the usual cruciform plan, it is now almost square,—in fact, the length from the reredos to the organ-screen is 132 feet, while the breadth across from the Latin Chapel to St. Lucy's Chapel is 108 feet. The church is made up of the shortened nave with its two aisles, and ante-chapel, the central tower, the north transept with its one aisle, the south transept, and the eastern half of the church, which itself contains no less than six divisions,—the choir, with its two aisles, the Lady Chapel on the north, and the Latin Chapel (or St. Catherine's) on the north again of that, while on the south is the small chapel of St. Lucy.

If the unusual appearance of the cathedral is partly due to Wolsey's destruction, it is partly due also to its being used as a college chapel, and partly to the fact that in general plan, and to some extent in detail, it is Ethelred's design, commenced seventy years before the great developments of Norman architecture began. Ethelred himself probably only completed the choir and adjacent parts, and even there the work was very much altered in late Norman times ; while the nave itself seems to be principally Norman (though built in imitation of Ethelred's work), with the exception of the pillars, which must be earlier than the Norman restoration, and may be of Saxon date, though we have no documentary clue as to what happened from the reign of Canute to that of Henry I., except that the church was, during the latter part of the time, in a very bad way.

The following are Mr. Park Harrison's conclusions as to the

general plan of the church, which he set before the British Archæological Association in 1892 :—"The design of the building is clearly derived from the original pre-Norman church. The uniformity of plan throughout affords a remarkable instance of the way in which early church-builders imitated previous work, the process being, at Oxford, slow enough to make stages in the construction, that must have occupied instead of thirty years, as stated in the explanatory cards suspended in the cathedral, and quoted in some of the guide-books, at least 160. There were three changes in the profiles of the bases, and three in the abaci, all before the years 1170 or 1180."

Thus the cathedral is a most important evidence of the high state of civilisation at which our Anglo-Saxon forefathers gradually arrived after the landing of St. Augustine. It is some satisfaction to our national pride to discover that they did not owe their culture to the Norman settlement, nor worship in wooden sheds before the arrival of the Conqueror, as was till recently supposed ; but that the people who produced poets like Cædmon, artists like Dunstan, and scholars like Alfred and Bede, were also able to build churches worthy of such great names. More will be said about their workmanship when we come to discuss the capitals in the choir, but here we may refer the reader to a drawing in Mr. Harrison's pamphlet, "The Pre-Norman Date," of the apse of a church from the "Dunstan" MS., which shows at what elaborate architecture the Anglo-Saxons had arrived by the year 1000, and illustrates the curious foliage found on the cathedral capitals.

The Nave was probably completed during the priorate of Robert of Cricklade (c. 1160–1180), the restoration being begun shortly after 1158, when the Pope's charter was secured. The clerestory, which is transitional, may therefore have been still unfinished at the time of his death.

The remarkable arrangement of the triforium is characteristic of all the four main divisions of the church. From the large pillars spring circular arches worked with heavy round mouldings. *Underneath* these arches, not above them, is the triforium which is a blind arcade of two arches set in the tympanum beneath the main arch. The reason why there is this space under the main arch is because corbels in the form of half-capitals are set on the further side of the great pillars, a good

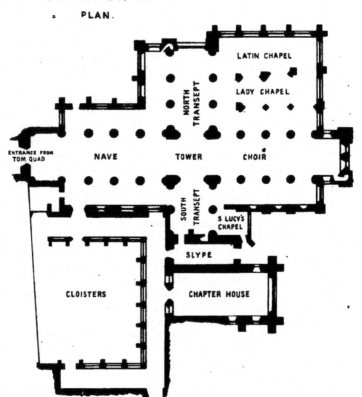

CHRISTCHURCH. OXFORD.

PLAN.

LATIN CHAPEL

NORTH TRANSEPT

LADY CHAPEL

ENTRANCE FROM
TOM QUAD

NAVE

TOWER

CHOIR

SOUTH TRANSEPT

S LUCY'S
CHAPEL

SLYPE

CLOISTERS

CHAPTER HOUSE

way below the true capitals, to support the vaulting of the aisles. In this way, says Scott, " the pillars and arches have been divided, as it were, into two halves in their thickness, the half facing the aisle retaining its natural height and proportions, but that facing the central space being so raised as to embrace the triforium stage, the openings of which appear between the two ranges of arches ; the clerestory ranging above." Of course, by this arrangement, the pillars avoid the low and stumpy proportions they would otherwise have, and the general effect of height in the nave (which is actually only 41 feet 6 inches) is considerably increased ; for, were the triforium in the usual place above the main arches, the main pillars would not come any higher than the lower half-capitals. The arrangement is very unusual in England ; though it is found in Italian Gothic, and even in Renaissance work in that country, as in St. Petronio, Bologna. It occurs in the transept of Romsey Abbey, in the choir at Jedburgh, in Dunstable Priory, and in Tewkesbury Abbey. That it existed in Saxon times is proved by a drawing in Cædmon's Paraphrase (c. 1000) in the Bodleian (c.f. "The Pre-Norman Date"). Dr. Ingram, who wrote in 1830, thought that this arrangement was made in order to raise the height of the building in the twelfth century, the triforium being the clerestory of the old Saxon church peeping out under the later work. And though his zeal was not according to knowledge (he thought the chapter-house doorway was Saxon), yet there is a possibility that this theory of his may have some truth in it.

Until lately, the church was thought to belong altogether to Prior Guimond's time. Sir Gilbert Scott fixed the date of the rather heavily carved capital over Bishop Berkeley's monument at 1170–80, owing to its close resemblance to certain capitals at Canterbury Cathedral of this period. The others seem to be of earlier date than this, and possibly of Ethelred's time. Strange as they are, however, they do not suggest a Saxon origin so strongly as do those of the choir. They are unique in design, and have neither the massiveness of Norman, nor the crisp severity of Early English work. The light, graceful, and rather fantastic foliage of the three eastern capitals on the south side—almost like iron-work—will be noticed. The third capital on the north side bears some resemblance to two of those in the choir.

The pillars of the nave also present problems of some difficulty. They are alternately circular and octagonal, and the masonry of six of them points with something like certainty to a date considerably earlier than the twelfth century restoration. In the four western pillars the stones are a good deal smaller than those in the two octagonal ones of the next bay : this makes it highly probable that they are of earlier date than the octagonal pillars, which are certainly Norman of the period

of the restoration c. 1160. Mr. Harrison believes there is also considerable evidence that the two cylindrical pillars were reduced in girth in order to make them of the same size as the octagonal pillars then introduced; for the lower half-capitals project nine inches on either side beyond the pillars, while in those of the choir,

EARLY ENGLISH MOULDING. which are unreduced, their projection is only five. There is also reason to suppose that the other pair of octagonal pillars, those by the organ-screen, were cut out of older ones at the same time.

The clerestory windows are transitional, as is proved among other things by their being pointed, for purely æsthetic reasons, and not (as in the case of the north and south tower-arches) from any structural necessity. Each window has a smaller blind arch on either side of it, making a triple opening within to a single window in the wall ; and the shafts of this triple opening are made to carry small attached shafts which bear the arches above. The capitals of the larger and lower shafts spread in an unusual manner, having to support a mass of walling.

The Roof is a fine example of sixteenth century wood-work, and doubtless replaced a simpler Norman roof of wood; but the brackets which support it were added later to the Norman shafts, in order to carry a Perpendicular vault of stone, which was never carried out. It is divided into small panels, whose ornament, though rich, is rather mechanical.

The nave and choir are used as the College Chapel of Christ Church. In the returned stalls by the organ-screen sit the two censors ; most of the undergraduates occupy the benches of the nave (which are modern wood-work carved by Chapman after

NAVE AND CHOIR, LOOKING EAST (*from a photograph by Carl Norman & Co.*).

Sir G. G. Scott's designs), as far as the raised seats where the choir sits; the central benches under the tower are reserved for the freshmen; while the dean, canons, students (*i.e.*, fellows), and graduates fill the stalls of the choir, the other seats of the choir being occupied by the Scholars. The public use the aisles, transepts, and chapels on Sundays, but on week-days are free of the nave for the two special cathedral services.

Monuments of the Nave.—Berkeley's monument is attached to one of the north pillars, which it entirely defaces. *George Berkeley* was Bishop of Cloyne, and died in 1753, during a visit to Oxford; he was as good as he was famous, and his monument is as large as it is ugly. The epitaph, though not altogether untrue, and doubtless well meant, has the unfortunate effect of prepossessing the reader against its subject,— *Si Christianus fueris, si amans patriae, utroque nomine gloriari potes Berkleium vixisse.* Beneath is inscribed the quotation from Pope,—

" To Berkeley every virtue under heaven."

On the pier by the pulpit the talented *Dean Aldrich* is commemorated by a bust, which shows him to have had a very good face, and bears by way of further adornment a winged skull that is quite unnecessarily hideous. Aldrich has been already referred to : he was the architect of Peckwater and All Saints, the composer of many well-known anthems and services, the author of the once standard "Oxford Logic," and "a most universal scholar." He succeeded Massey, the Roman Catholic dean, who had to "make off and retire across the seas" in 1689. Browne Willis says of Aldrich that "as he spent his Days in Celibacy, so he appropriated his Income to Hospitality and Generosity, and, like Bishop Fell, always encouraged learning ; as a celebrated Author tells us, 'to the utmost of his Power, being one of the greatest then in England, if we consider him as a Christian, or a Gentleman,' to which give me leave to add that he always had the Interest of his College at heart ; of which I may experimentally say, he was an excellent Governor." He was very modest, and desired to be buried without any memorial, a wish which was at first complied with by his "thrifty nephew." Sunk into a pillar opposite is a curious old brass, to the memory of John Walrond, student, who died young in 1602.

A marble slab on the pavement in the midst of the nave commemorates *Dr. Pusey*, who was canon of Christ Church, in virtue of his Hebrew Professorship, and lies buried here. The Latin inscription mentions also his wife and daughter, and of him it speaks as "Professor of the Hebrew tongue, and Canon of this church (*aedis*), who in the peace and pity of Jesus fell asleep, September 16th, 1882, being 82 years and 24 days old."

The Organ stands on a fine Jacobean screen, dating from Duppa's time (c. 1635); it was removed here from before the

PULPIT.

choir during the restoration. The outer casing belonged to a former organ built by Father Schmidt in 1680. The present instrument was built by Willis & Son in 1884. It has four manuals and pedals, thirty-nine speaking stops, nine couplers, ten pneumatic pistons, six composition pedals, and other accessory movements. It has a very fine tone, and is well placed for sound. Its external appearance is much improved by the pretty green *appliqué* curtain which now hangs in front of the organist's seat.

The Pulpit.—Christ Church is fortunate in possessing an old oak pulpit, escaping thus the garish ventures in marble which have been disastrous to so many other cathedrals. This pulpit is Jacobean (c. 1635). It is a remarkable piece of workmanship, elaborately carved, and well designed : the grotesques on the panels should be especially noticed, as well as the light elevated canopy, surmounted by a pelican, which was at one time transferred to the episcopal throne, and has recently been restored to its original use.

The Tower is not square, the nave and choir sides being wider than those of the transepts. For this practical reason (and not because of the transitional character of the work, though transitional it is) the north and south arches are pointed, while the east and west are round-headed. The tower arches seem originally to have sprung from the imposts ornamented with trefoil leaves which can still be seen, though they were cut

CHOIR AND NAVE, LOOKING WEST.

through when the present capitals were introduced at the time
of the Norman restoration. The Norman shafts and capitals
were attached to the older and ruder piers. Round these piers
are the shafts of very firm and graceful proportions, their
capitals decorated with foliage. The lower parts of the vaulting
shafts of the great piers are cut off and finished with a narrow
beading, which shows that the ritual choir originally stood here,
and did not correspond with the structural choir.

The lantern, which had been blocked up, was reopened at the
time of the recent improvements, and adds considerably to the
appearance of the church. Its first stage is ornamented with
an arcade of stout Norman shafts, whose capitals are carved
with a breadth and simplicity well suited to the height at which
they stand : the arcade is bounded above and below by a heavy
round string course. The upper stage has another arcade,
of four large round arches on each side, the corner ones
pierced as windows. Above is an early sixteenth century roof :
it is divided into square panels, in most of which marks of the
old ornaments (in the form of Maltese crosses like those of the
nave roof) can be clearly discerned. At the springing of the
main arches Fifteenth Century corbels have been inserted. In
the south-east pier of the tower occurs the break in the
masonry which marks, it is thought, the cessation of the
building operations when Ethelred was driven out of England
by Sweyn. It can be clearly seen from the south choir aisle.
The tooling of the masonry half way up the tower has also
been found to be marked with the cross lines, which dis-
tinguish Saxon from Norman mason's work.

During Mr. Billing's restoration in 1856 a remarkable crypt
was opened three feet beneath the paving of the choir between
the north and south piers of the tower. This crypt, which was
covered up again after investigation, was 7 feet long by 5 feet
6 inches, and just high enough for a man to stand upright ; its
walls were of stone, and contained aumbries or lockers at each
end. There were also slight remains of indented crosses on the
western side, and at the east enough was missing to suggest a
doorway. The entrance to this chamber may have been
through a trap-door, or by a passage leading into the east side.
It was clearly not intended for sepulture, as its length was from
north to south ; and the absence of passages giving convenient
access on each side seems to prove that it was not intended

for the exhibition of relics.   The most likely theory is that it was used as a secret chamber to contain the University chest, which was called the Frideswide chest, because it was kept in a secure place in this church, its keys being in the hands of certain canons by appointment of the chancellor.   If this seems a very public place for a secret chamber, it must be remembered that originally it was immediately under the rood-loft, and therefore admitted of a trap-door being concealed ; though the resting-place of the chest may not have been kept very secret for all we know.   This crypt was probably made in Norman times, and is unique of its kind.

The Aisles of the Nave and Transepts show the progress which was made at the end of the twelfth century in vaulting : Mr. Ruskin says of the work here that it is " bad and rude enough, but the best we could do with our own wits, and no French help."   Vaulting originally began with square ribs, afterwards the ribs became plain half-rounds, and later were moulded. Here we find good specimens of the development of all three stages.   In the choir aisles the vaulting arches are partly square and the ribs on the groins half-round, of a heavy character. These ribs were inserted at a later period, as is sufficiently clear from the awkward way they are fitted to corbels at the side of the capitals which carry the vault.   In the west aisle of the north transept the vaulting is the same, but lighter in character ; and there are no corbels, though the fitting is still awkward. In the north aisle of the nave the vaulting is pointed but still with plain half-round ribs, a little lighter than in the transept-aisles.   But in the south aisle of the nave, as the builders got on with their work to the westward, their style underwent a further development, and a pear-shaped moulding with a fillet along the edge proclaims that the Early English period had begun. With the completion of this aisle they seemed to have become bolder ; for the vaulting shafts in the transepts with their unmistakable Norman capitals, and the solitary ribbed stones resting on those of the south transept, prove that they intended to go beyond the practice of Norman architects and throw a vault across the wider span of the transepts themselves. Perhaps they immediately afterwards discovered that the task was beyond them : at all events the vaulting shafts were left as they are, and the transepts have never been vaulted.

The windows of the nave and transept aisles are uniformly

uninteresting. They were originally plain Norman lights, then Perpendicular, then seventeenth century Gothic, and finally "restored" by Scott, in imitation of the Perpendicular work. The windows of Dean Duppa, which they replaced, were certainly not beautiful in their tracery, as may be seen by that at the west end of the north nave aisle, which only the delightful Dutch glass of Van Ling redeems,—but they at least had some character. In the south nave aisle an attempt has been made to hark further back by the introduction of a window in Norman style; but fortunately this has not been persevered with. Only one of the original Romanesque windows remains, by which to judge the effect contemplated by the first architects; it is that containing Bishop King's portrait.

Glass in the Aisles.—The glass in the restored Perpendicular windows of the nave aisles (by Clayton and Bell) is very unsatisfactory both in colour and design. Of that in the round-headed window of the south aisle of the nave by an Irish artist (O'Connor) one can only say that it was better conceived than executed. Over the door that leads into the cloister is a half-window by Mr. Wailes.

The "Faith, Hope, and Charity" window next to this (namely, at the west end of the aisle) was Sir Edward Burne Jones' second essay here in this craft. If his first, that in St. Catherine's, the Latin Chapel, was a wonderful success, this one is a not unpleasant failure, but a failure none the less. None of the figures are very graceful; the firing seems to have gone wrong in the most important places, especially in the faces, which are coarse and expressionless, though one cannot help admiring the fortitude of Charity in carrying the bulky infant who presents his vast back to the spectator. The colour is strong, and free from the miserable timidity of the work in the Perpendicular windows,—for the whole thing is of course a work of art (and not of commerce), though an unsuccessful one, —still it fails to harmonise. The window as a whole, however, is saved by the beautiful foliage which forms the background, and by the four slender figures in the tracery.

Others have admired it more. Here, for instance, is an appreciative description from the columns of "The Builder" for April 1888:—"The figure of Hope has a greyish-blue drapery, varied in tint, and diapered with the pattern of a flower in stain. The scarf floating round the figure is sky-blue in tone, and lighter than the dress. The figure of Charity has a ruby over-mantle, with a white dress underneath; while the figure of Faith has a blue dress beautifully and richly diapered, the upper portion with a sumptuous Venetian design familiar on the brocades of the sixteenth century, and the lower portion with a sprig of foliage. The tone of the backgrounds is a rich, warm green, and is very carefully painted with foliage, and the contrast yielded by the pale blue of the drapery, and the rich, warm green of the background in the two outside windows, is most harmonious and striking. The detail in this window is very elaborate, and every part of it bears traces of care and thought."

In a corner of this window is an inscription,—*In Memoriam Edwardi Denison hujusce Aedis commensalis Curâ amicorum,* A.D. *1870.* Edward Denison, nephew of the Speaker, and son of the Bishop of Salisbury, was the pioneer of those who have since founded the numerous settlements in the neglected parts of London. At a period of acute distress he convinced himself that no good could be done by sending money from the West End unless educated people could be found who would give up their lives to making friends with the poor. Accordingly he took the novel step of going to live in the East End; there he founded a club, and lived apart from the brilliant society to which he was accustomed. Besides teaching and organising, he studied carefully the social conditions of his neighbours, and many of the methods now universally practised date from his experience. Shortly after he had been elected M.P. for Newark he died, at the early age of twenty-nine, and there was "hardly a home within his district that had not some memory left of the love and tenderness of his personal charity."

In the west end of the north aisle of the nave is the last remaining relic of the glass which the Dutchman Van Ling painted in Dean Duppa's time. The rest, which filled the aisle, was removed about twenty-five years since, on the ground that it made the church too dark. There are various opinions about this window, which represents Jonah sitting under his gourd, and the town of Nineveh in the distance. We must confess to a great admiration for it; the foliage is fine and rich, and if it is a little over-strong in its green, that only makes it more characteristic of its age. And, however that may be, there cannot be two opinions as to beauty of the town in the background, which reminds one irresistibly of Dürer; and, with its rich brown houses, bluish roofs, touches of greenery, and fair purple hills beyond, make the right-hand light of the window a picture of which one never wearies. The whole is leaded in rectangular panes, like Bishop King's window.

Monuments of the Nave Aisles.—In the south aisle there are two monuments of interest; that of *Corbet* (1688) for the characteristic decoration of cupids and wreath work; that of *Pococke* for further reasons. Edward Pococke (1604–1691), whose bust was moved here from the north aisle by Scott, is represented with pointed beard and wearing the old tufted college cap. He was the great Arabic scholar of his day; the first text in Hebrew characters printed at Oxford was published by him, and his 420 oriental MSS. were bought by the University. Yet he was condemned, under the Commonwealth, by the Berkshire "Committee of Scandalous Ministers," on the ground of "insufficiency," his real offence being that he had used part of the Prayer Book in the public service. There are two portraits of him in the Bodleian, representing him with light hair and dark eyes; and a fig-tree which he planted still flourishes on the south side of the Professor of Hebrew's house. A striking biography of him has come down to us in a sentence —" His life appeared to me one constant calm."

The North Transept has the unnoticeable peculiarity, that it turns slightly westward. This is because the choir (into which it is built at right angles) turns a little to the north, to symbolise, it is said, the droop of our Lord's head upon the cross. The western aisle of this transept still remains; the eastern aisle has been lost in the chapels, of which it now forms the respective western bays.

The north bay of this transept bears the marks in its clerestory of late Perpendicular restoration; the carved heads on the string-course above the arch afford an interesting comparison with the Norman heads above the capitals, and are vigorous sketches of contemporary life. The capitals in this transept and those in the north aisle of the nave are strong and varied. The wooden roof of both the transepts was made in the early sixteenth century, earlier than that of the nave.

The tracery of the great north window had been altered and made ugly by the seventeenth century restorers; it was accordingly restored back to its original design by Sir Gilbert Scott.

F

Under this north window is a panelled tomb belonging to Henry VII.'s time. It is attributed to *James Zouch*, a monk of the priory, who died in 1503. In his will, dated October 16, 1503, and preserved in the Prerogative Office in London, he directs that he shall be interred under the window of the north transept, and a tomb be erected for him in the midst of the same window. He also bequeathed £30 to the convent for vaulting that part of the church, in consideration of his being there buried.

On each of the shields in the quatrefoil compartments of the tomb is an inkhorn and pen-case, indicating, it is said, that the monk was a notary or scribe by profession, though Dr. Ingram speaks of "the pen-case and inkhorn of Zouch" as an heraldic blazonry.

In the north transept aisle there are curious thin, wavy scrolls of brasses, commemorating "Leonardus Hutton," and hard by are two pleasant kneeling figures also in brasses.

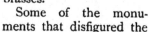
FROM THE NORTH TRANSEPT.

Some of the monuments that disfigured the church have fortunately been removed; of these is Chantrey's great sitting figure of Cyril Jackson, which took up most of the north transept, but is now removed to the Library. Of these sequestrated monuments some have been placed in the ante-chapel; among them are the large and simple memorial of Bishop Fell, and those of Dean Gaisford (d. 1855) and Bishop Lloyd (d. 1829).

One cannot but admire the spirit which has caused so many brasses to be set up in recent years to deceased members of the House; and yet it has become an abuse which calls for serious protest. It is now so much a precedent that every member of the foundation should have a brass set up to his memory at his death, that the tribute is become mechanical, and indeed it would now be a marked slight if any don should die without a memorial brass being erected. At this rate the cathedral will in a few generations be entirely defaced unless the tradition be interrupted. As it is, the brasses are all the reverse of beautiful ; and, after a period of lacquered obtrusiveness, they become leprous, and afterwards black. A modern brass, indeed, defaces a wall as much as a modern tablet. Surely some more beautiful form of memorial could be devised. The cathedral is in need of many things, of colour, and hangings, and furniture. Could not those tributes of respect take in the future this more honourable form ? Then, when an inscription is necessary, the enamelled tablet, with its endless possibilities of jewel-like colour, might be used in place of brass or marble. Something has already been done by the erection of the beautiful eastern windows, and the cathedral has been fortunate in escaping an eruption of episcopal tombs ; but latterly there has been an epidemic of brasses, which makes one fear that the artist's work is being forgotten in the temptation to set off an epitaph with a display of Latinity.

Glass in the Transepts.—The great window of the north transept is by Clayton and Bell. Mr. Tyrwhitt says of it that it " glows with all the fires which a fervid fancy can bestow upon the inwards of the Dragon."

The glaring glass in the clerestory of the north and south transepts is by Henri and Alfred Gérente (1854), artists famous in their day. It was originally in the great east window (now destroyed), and must have thrown the members of the House into a stupor when in that prominent position. As it is, the clerestory windows are a very inappropriate place for colour, violent enough to " scare a chameleon " ; though the glass was evidently put there as the least conspicuous position. It might now be taken out and buried, on the chance that time and the earth may have a mellowing effect.

The half-window above the vestry in the south transept is filled with glass, coloured to look as if it were old, by Clayton and Bell, and given in memory of Dr. Liddon.

The South Transept was originally on the same plan as the north, but its aisles have disappeared : that on the west to

make room for the cloister ; while that on the east is now represented by the chapel of St. Lucy. Its appearance has also
been much altered by the division of its southern bay into two

SAXON CLERESTORY WINDOW IN SOUTH TRANSEPT (*from a drawing
by J. Park Harrison*).

stories, which reduces its length, since the lower story is the slype
or passage that leads from the cloister to the cemetery, and is

therefore to all intents and purposes outside the church.. The upper story is reached by steps from the transept floor. The whole of this curious structure, which has the appearance of a small house built into the transept, is a modern restoration, its immediate predecessor having been literally a house where dwelt the verger and his family. In earlier times, however, there had been some kind of erection here, which was used as a sacristy, and of this traces were found by Gilbert Scott which led to the present restoration. As these traces, however, consisted principally of some fragments of a staircase, the present Early English restoration is only conjectural. On the whole it is tolerable, though the heavy and unnecessary central buttress one may well suppose not to be part of the old design. Why the slope of this buttress, which stands in the middle of the transept, should be so stoutly protected against the weather, it is hard to imagine. The carving on the tympanum over the door that leads into the slype is stiff and repulsive. Just · to the right of this door is a holy water stoup, very simply cut into the pillar, which proves that this entrance from the slype was usual in old times, when the monastic buildings lay on that side of the church ; at present, however, the door is commonly kept locked.

The chamber above the slype, representing the old sacristy, is now used as a vestry. It is reached from the transept, and a staircase in it leads to the gallery above, whence in all probability a door led straight into the dormitory of the monastery. A similar arrangement to this existed at Bristol, which was also an Augustinian house ; and there are traces of a door in the wall of Canon Sanday's house which further substantiate the conjecture. Some direct access to the church from the dormitory was a great convenience in the days when matins was said in the middle of the night.

The gallery is now used as a kind of museum for any odd fragments that are discovered in the precincts. Among them is the quaintly carved base of a Norman cross, which before the Reformation stood, together with a pulpit, at the west end of the nave, near the place now occupied by the fountain. The subjects represented are the Fall, Abraham's Sacrifice, the Giving of the Law.

The open triforium directly over the Lyttleton monument in this transept is an important relic of the second Saxon church, and a good instance of the slight things which sometimes turn the scales in antiquarian disputes. Professor Willis had in 1840 pronounced (as against Dr. Ingram, whose pet theory it was that the triforium was the clerestory of Ethelred's church) that the triforium must be of Norman design, because no grooves could be found for the insertion of glass in the shafts, as would be the case if it were Saxon.

Mr. Harrison accordingly, in December 1891, made a close examination of the shaft and small arches in the open triforium which had struck him as of Saxon character, with the result that the grooves for glass were discovered to exist beyond a doubt, but so neatly stopped with mortar as previously to have escaped notice. They can be clearly discerned inside the arches, by anyone with good sight, from the floor of the church. The base of the shaft which carries these arches is equally decisive, for it is "pudding shaped," entirely different from the other bases, and most unmistakably Saxon: it also can be seen from the floor, but is worth an inspection from the gallery over the choir-vestry, whence there is also an impressive view of the church. With this exception, the triforia and clerestories of the transepts are similar to those of the nave, though Saxon tooling has been found on the wall, and there is a break in some of the masonry on the angle shaft near the vestry door, which possesses a Saxon base. The principal arches of the clerestories are not pointed, which proves that the transepts were rebuilt earlier than the nave. Two corbels on the east side of the transept mark the site of a musicians' gallery which once projected beyond the triforium.

St. Lucy's Chapel in the second bay of the old south transept aisle was used as a vestry in the days when the transept was devoted to domestic purposes. It must have ruined the effect of this part of the church, and formed an extremely inconvenient vestry. Now the chapel is used, not very appropriately, as a baptistery; it contains a font, well designed and carved, which was executed in 1882. It is Norman or earlier, with the exception of the eastern wall, which was rebuilt in order to hold the present beautiful window. This window is of an uncommon type; the three lights, less than half the height of the tracery above them, commence considerably below the spring of the arch. The tracery, which reminds one of that in Dorchester Abbey, a few miles away, is flamboyant in character, suggesting the form which the decadence of Gothic architecture took in France; only in this case it is a decadence that is vigorous as well as graceful.

The chapel recalls the time when King Charles held his court in Christ Church, at the time of the Civil War, many cavalier knights being buried here.

Monuments of the South Transept and Chapel.— There are the tombs of several prominent royalists in the transept as well as in St. Lucy's little chapel, most of which might well be spared were it not for their historic interest. That of Viscount Grandison, for instance, consists of an urn on a pedestal, altogether huge and hideous; yet Grandison was a brave and doubtless a graceful cavalier, who died in Oxford of wounds received in the attack on Bristol in 1643. Another ugly, big monument is that of Sir E. Littleton, keeper of the Great Seal, who took up arms "for the royal majesty, during the execrable siege of this city." Sir John Smith is also buried here : he "redeemed the banner royal" at the battle of Edge-hill, was knighted on the field by the King, and died of his wounds in 1644, at the early age of twenty-eight.

A very odd monument is that to Viscount Brouncker, who died in 1645, having been chamberlain to the young Charles, then Prince of Wales. A smartly dressed gentleman and his wife are represented seated in meditative attitudes, each with an elbow on the table, while between their two elbows is propped a skull.

In the tracery of St. Lucy's chapel is to be found the finest old glass in the cathedral. It belongs to the year 1330, or thereabouts, and enables one to imagine what the church must have looked like when glass of this magnificent description abounded, and hangings and· altar-pieces and wall-paintings, hardly less rich, filled every conspicuous position. In the uppermost compartment of the tracery is a figure of our Lord seated in glory ; below there are angels with censers, and next two Augustinian monks in blue and white robes, kneeling with outstretched arms ; then come coats of arms, and various grotesque beasts, all most richly coloured in ruby and blue and green and gold. Below, in the principal spaces, are (1) St. Martin on horseback giving his coat to the beggar ; (2) the martyrdom of St. Thomas à Becket: St. Thomas' head has been knocked out by some fanatic, and replaced with white

glass ; the armour and shields of the knights should be noticed ;
(3) St. Augustine, who holds a pastoral staff, is teaching his
monks and others.   In the next four spaces are :—The head of
a king ; St. Cuthbert, carrying the head of St. Oswald, and
wearing a green chasuble ; St. Blaise, in a mulberry-coloured
chasuble ; the head of a queen.   The glass in the three main
lights was destroyed, and then replaced by some of seventeenth
century work, but this too is now gone, all except a portion of

THIRD CAPITAL OF CHOIR.

the upper part, which shows that the design was architectural
in character, and the colour that of fog-smitten stone-work.
    The Choir is in four bays with a presbytery ; it is in the
same style as the rest of the church, with the exception of the
Perpendicular alterations in the upper part.   It was formerly
filled with heavy, ugly wood-work, and half way up all the pillars
may be traced the modern stone-work which had to be inserted
when the stalls and panelling that had encased the pillars were
removed.   Not a wreck of the old wood remains, and the choir
is now seated with walnut-wood stalls by Farmer and Brindley,

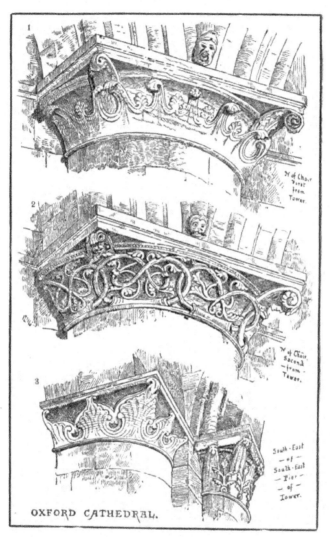

1

2

N of Choir
First
from
Tower.

N of Choir.
Second
— from —
Tower.

3

South-East
— of —
South-East
— Pier —
— of —
Tower.

OXFORD CATHEDRAL.

CAPITALS OF THE CHOIR (*from a drawing by J. Park Harrison*).

along which runs a light iron screen, very carefully wrought by Skidmore of Birmingham in 1871. It is copied from Queen Eleanor's tomb in Westminster Abbey. The pavement relaid in 1871 contains representations of the cardinal virtues, copied from the church of the Knights of St. John at Malta. Yet there were original artists to be found twenty-five years ago !

The pillars of the choir are larger than those of the nave, which appear to have been reduced in girth (see p. 54). They are (it is now generally admitted) part of Ethelred's church, dating from the first decade of the eleventh century ; but their bases belong to the Norman restoration, and were probably put in by Cricklade. The triforium is also Late Norman, here as throughout the church, with the single exception of the one window in the south transept.

But it is in the capitals of the choir that the most striking evidence of Saxon work in the church lies. Thus they are of remarkable interest, besides being very fine specimens of stone-carving. If the visitor sits in a stall in the middle of the south side of the choir he will have the three most important capitals before him, and can study them at leisure. One striking feature common to them all is that they bear very evident traces of having been worn by the weather. It has been found by Mr. Drinkwater that the stone of which they are made is too durable to have been affected by the atmosphere while under cover. This proves that they must have been in their present position exposed to the driving rains from the south, during the long period when the church was in ruins, that is to say, before the restoration of the twelfth century.

Another significant feature which these three capitals have in common, not only with each other but with all the others in the choir, is that their abaci are extremely thick, just twice as thick as those in the transepts and nave ; and thick abaci are a mark of early work.

Their ornamentation is remarkable, partly Saxon and partly oriental in character, and quite unlike any Norman work. Sir Gilbert Scott himself noticed the latter characteristic of these and other capitals in the church. "The foliated ornament," he wrote, "assumes a noble character, evidently evincing a study of the ancient Greek, which was effected through a Byzantine medium." We have already seen, in the History of the Cathedral, how this Byzantine influence is to be accounted for by the fact that Greek clergy flocked to the court of Ethelred's brother-in-law Richard ; and further, it must be noted that many illuminated MSS. of Saxon date show that Greek ornament was admired and studied at the time. Professor Westwood, in his "*Lapidarium,*" points out that in Saxon art the designs of stone-carving are so completely identical with those in the MSS. as to lead us to suppose that the artists of the illuminated drawings were also the designers of the architecture. So much is this the case that, "the age of a particular MS. being ascertained, we are able approximately to determine also the age of the carving." Professor Westwood was, in fact, among the first to be convinced of the Saxon origin of the capitals we are discussing.

It is worth while to give a few illustrations of this very important point. The first capital from the tower on the north side of the choir is ornamented with that curious *spuma* or wave-shaped work which has just the dip and swing of a wave of the sea as it curls over before breaking.

In a Psalter of the beginning of the eleventh century (B. M. Har. 2904) is to be found precisely the same vivid conventionalism.*

The second capital is the most curious one in the church, and is also the most strikingly Saxon, the stalks issuing from pipes or tubes being as characteristic almost of Saxon as interlaced work is of Celtic art.

Standing immediately under this capital, one is able clearly to discern the faces on the corner volutes, which have each a crown of leaves like one found in the famous tenth century "Dunstan" MS. in the British Museum. One of these faces is that of a man, very heavy and stupid-looking ; the other that of a comely woman. It is not fanciful to suppose that they are portraits of the blundering Ethelred and his wife Emma.

The third capital is decorated with some branching work hardly less curious, and above it is a head wearing the unbifurcated mitre, which dropped out of use in the eleventh century. Of the three capitals on the south side of the choir, which do

* Mr. Park Harrison has collected some very interesting drawings from various Anglo-Saxon MSS., which afford striking parallels to the ornament on these and other capitals in the church. A reproduction of the drawing here referred to, and of others equally important, will be found in his " Pre-Norman Date."

not bear the same signs of weathering, one has branching work, and the other two reworked leafage, such as is found also in one on the north side of the nave.

As for the triforium and the rest of the work of the choir, it was all so much restored in the twelfth century that one cannot find in it any traces of Ethelred's work.

The pendent roof is one of the most striking features of the cathedral, and is worth careful study. Fergusson considers this roof to be the most satisfactory attempt ever made to surmount the great difficulty presented in all fan-tracery by the awkward, flat, central space which is left in each bay by the four cones of the vault. At Gloucester, King's College Chapel, Cambridge, Henry VII.'s Chapel, Westminster, and other places, various attempts were made to deceive the eye, and hide the unmanageable space; in Henry VII.'s Chapel the well-known pendants were boldly introduced with this object. None were wholly satisfactory, but, says Fergusson :—

"Strange as it may appear from its date, the most satisfactory roof of this class is that erected by Cardinal Wolsey in the beginning of the sixteenth century [this is a mistake, the roof having been built some time before] over the choir of Oxford Cathedral. In this instance the pendants are thrust so far forward, and made so important, that the central part of the roof is practically quadripartite. The remaining difficulty was obviated by abandoning the circular, horizontal outline of true fan-tracery, and adopting a polygonal form instead. As the whole is done in a constructive manner and with appropriate detail, this roof, except in size, is one of the best and most remarkable ever executed."

Fan-tracery is a peculiarly English feature, and was invented, according to Fergusson, in order to get rid of the endless repetition of inverted pyramids which earlier vaulting produced. He therefore considers it an improvement on the vaulting of the early English and Decorated periods; and, as he thinks the roof of Christ Church Cathedral to be the best example of fan-tracery, he comes near to pronouncing it the finest ceiling in the world.

It certainly must strike every observer as possessing exceptional beauty. At once rich and light, it yet accords wonderfully with the homely Norman work that it crowns, and gives a happy finish to the most important part of the cathedral.

Even the lantern pendants seem more graceful than is usually the case with those strange architectural solecisms. Mr. Ruskin calls the roof "true Tudor grotesque, inventively constructive, delicately carved, summing the builder's skill in the fifteenth century."

The roof is certainly too early in design to have been built by

TRACERY OF THE ROOF.

Wolsey, as was supposed. But there are traces in the work which have led some antiquaries to suppose that, though begun about 1480, its western bay may not have been finished till the Cardinal's time, or even till the end of Henry's reign. The head on the large corbel over the Dean's stall certainly

wears a Tudor crown, and is bearded. This would lead one to
suppose it to be a likeness of Henry VIII. : furthermore, the
face is broad but emaciated, with the beard straggling ; and
we learn from historians that the King did let his beard grow
longer at the end of his life, when he was worn and ill, and
expressed more penitence for his many misdeeds than he is
generally given credit for. The woman's head on the corbel
opposite, also wearing a Tudor crown, would probably be the
last of his wives, Katherine Parr. The face wears the happy
expression of one delivered from great anxiety.

In the arched space nearly above these heads are four
canopied figures : on the north, St. Peter with his keys, and St.
Mary Magdalen (suggestive of Wolsey's own college in
Oxford) ; on the south St. Luke, over his bull (possibly because
of the connection of St. Frideswide's with the healing art), and
St. Catherine, holding the remains of a sword in her right
hand, and retaining a fragment of the wheel in her left. St.
Katherine will be found in the same attitude in a painted
window of the Latin Chapel. The central bosses of the roof
are interesting. Over the altar is the head of our Lord, surrounded by an aureole, the beard twisted into three points : in
the next bay is the Madonna and Child, and next a graceful
figure, identified as St. Frideswide by the curious sceptre with
heavy foliage at the end, which she is again represented with in
the middle window of the Latin Chapel. An angel is on either
side of this figure. In the next bay is an archbishop (Augustine ?) with his cross ; and on the last a bishop (perhaps
Birinus), holding his pastoral staff and supported by two
figures which may be chaplains or acolytes.

The clerestory of the choir was converted into Perpendicular
at the time when the roof was vaulted. The old walls were
simply covered with panelling, and the old windows enlarged
into Perpendicular ones.

The East End, now one of the most characteristic features
of the cathedral, is the work of Sir G. Gilbert Scott, and is
supposed to be a reproduction of the original twelfth century
design : for enough fragments of the old work were said to
remain on the walls to leave no doubt as to its original plan.
Of course the detail has the usual machine-made look of
modern carving ; but it is something to have recovered the
original effect, especially as the Decorated window which it has

replaced had been spoilt in the seventeenth century, when it was altered from its original five lights to three. The design, says Mr. J. H. Parker, is very rare in England, and not common anywhere. It consists of a large wheel-window, with an intersecting arcade under it, and *two* round-headed windows below : the wheel-window is set in a large round arch that seems to rest on two stout pillars. This round window is an imitation of an old one in Canterbury Cathedral. The arcade has a truer and less mechanical look than most of the restored work. The whole effect of the East End is excellent ; dignified and varied, it has something of that refined homeliness which is so strong a characteristic of the cathedral. The stained glass in the windows by Clayton and Bell is not at all unpleasing when seen from a distance. It is in character with the stone-work, and only just fails to be really fine in colour. Dr. Liddon and Sir John Mowbray were the donors of the glass.

It was formerly thought that the Norman presbytery was part of the original choir, and therefore presumably the earliest portion of the church ; but Mr. Harrison gives the following technical reasons for holding that it was an addition to an older building with an apse, built by Ethelred :—

1. The arches of the two side windows cut through string courses which run eastwards on both sides of the presbytery, being, in fact, continuations of the abaci proper of the half-capitals at that end of the choir. 2. If the east windows were designed from fragments of previously existing Norman ones, these cannot have been of the same date as the choir arches. The mouldings are later, and the old bases of the windows still in the east wall are clearly of transitional character, differing essentially from those belonging to corner shafts in the east aisles of the transepts. 3. The east walls of the choir aisles, which had been heightened to carry the vaulting, abut against and cover the jambs of the two side windows of the presbytery on the outside, a thing which could not have happened had the presbytery and choir aisles formed part of the same design.

The Reredos, an anonymous gift, erected in 1881 in red Dumfries sandstone, is a pleasant contrast to the chilly erections which now deface so many of our cathedrals. It has been said to be " perhaps the most exquisite piece of modern workmanship in Oxford," though this would not necessarily be very high praise. But, though a little too small for its position, a little wanting in breadth and overstrained in detail, it is a sound and sincere piece of work. Nor can we agree with the criticism which says that nothing can make it look like part of the structure, for this is the fault of the structure in its present condition ; when the old colouring is revived, the reredos will certainly not be too rich for it, and there is plenty of late Gothic in the choir to harmonise with its carving. Mr. Bodley designed it, and Mr. Brindley was the sculptor of the figures. They are of marble (rosso antico), and are excellent both in feeling and execution. The central panel represents the Crucifixion, with Our Lady and St. John at the foot of the cross, and Jerusalem in the background. In the niches on the left are St. Michael in armour, and St. Stephen in a dalmatic ; on the right, St. Augustine, in cope and mitre, and a very feminine looking St. Gabriel. Above the niches are carved and gilt shields bearing the emblems of the Passion. The warm effect of the whole is heightened by two handsome, green curtains on either side. The inscription under the crucifix is *Per crucem tuam libera nos Domine.*

The High Altar, of cedar wood, is less successful. Its eight clumsy legs, which are the only part visible, are covered with unpleasant, geometrical carving, most inappropriately accentuated by gilding : the result is that an impression of some strange, many-legged insect fastens on one in entering the church, and is hard to dislodge. One could wish that the altar were panelled, or frontals used to cover the legs.

The two silver-gilt candlesticks are extremely fine examples of seventeenth century plate ; they are rather squat in shape, with large bases richly embossed. The alms-dish which stands over the credence is also silver-gilt of the same date, magnificently embossed. These were given at the Restoration, and bear the date 1661–2. The chalices, patens, and flagons have been made to match them in more recent times. The altar books are good specimens of binding in velvet and precious metal. They were given in 1638 by Canon Henry King. On the fly-leaf of each book is a curious inscription in Latin, of which the following is a translation :—" Bequeathed to the Church of Christ, Oxford. A brand snatched from the burning, 1647, by the zealous care of R. Gardiner, Canon of Ch. Ch., but displaced from his rightful position by the greed of his times." These books were in use when Charles I. worshipped in the cathedral during the civil war.

The lectern, of ancient, pale brass enriched with filigree work, and garnished with amethyst, cornelian, and agate stones, is the gift of two former censors of the House, the Rev. T. Vere Bayne and the Rev. H. L. Thompson. The stem, sur-mounted by a globe and a good conventional eagle, bears the figures of St. Frideswide, Cardinal Wolsey, and Bishop King. At the base are three lions bearing the arms of the Priory, the College, and the University. The bible bears the date 1674. A beautifully illuminated lectionary on vellum, a relic of Cardinal Wolsey, and used by him in this church, can be seen in the Christ Church library.

The Bishop's Throne (in Italian walnut) is a not very inspired. work of Messrs. Farmer and Brindley. It was put up as a memorial to Bishop Wilberforce, at a cost of £1000, and has a medallion of the Bishop with mitre and pastoral staff at the back.

The South Choir Aisle is of an earlier period than the nave and transept aisles, the walls being, it is thought, of Ethelred's time. A stone bench runs along its south side, adding to its bright and pleasant appearance. The southern windows were rebuilt by Scott in Norman style of a different character to the window containing Bishop King's portrait which has its original capitals and bases. The corbels which carry the vault are carved into heads of men and baboons : the vaulting ribs have been unmistakably fitted on to the earlier Norman work. The Decorated east window, which, owing to the Burne Jones glass, is such a prominent feature of the cathedral, is restored, but there is a good deal of the original ball-flower moulding around it. At the side is a late Perpendicular piscina, with bold, square flowers cut on the jambs ; and on the pillars opposite there are traces of paintings, which must have been very bright-coloured once, and would very likely be so still, had it not been for Brian Duppa's wood-work.

Monuments.—There is an old brass on the wall, near the eastern end, to Stephen Pence, who died in 1587. Near this is a not very pleasing life-size medallion of Prince Leopold in statuary marble set in Sicilian marble ; it was sculptured by Mr. T. Williamson of Esher. The bronze tablet, with the

G

portrait in relief of Dr. Mackarness, the late Bishop, is very much better both in colour and design.   Further west another medallion in statuary marble, set in giallo antico, commemorates Sarah Acland, the wife of Sir Henry Acland, who is a student of the House, and Regius Professor of Medicine in the University; the Sarah Acland Home for Nurses keeps her pious memory fresh in Oxford.

The late Tudor monument to the first Bishop of Oxford, *Robert King*, has been removed from its former place under his window to the bay between the aisle and St. Lucy's Chapel, where it now forms a sort of small screen to the little chapel. Bishop King died in 1577; his tomb is recessed, canopied, and covered with shallow panel-work in minute divisions, but without any effigy, sculptured or incised.   Though it is among the last works of the mediæval school of monumental architecture, it is still graceful and restrained; and indeed a great contrast to the new style of monument which came in a few years later.   *Inscription :—Hic jacet Robertus King sacre theologie Professor et primus Ep'us Oxon. qui obiit quarto die Decembris Anno (Domini M.D. LVII).*

Crossing to the north side of the choir, one reaches the beautiful cluster of chapels which add so much to the grace of the cathedral, relieving it of any grimness of aspect which its unbroken array of massive columns might otherwise have produced, and by their unaffected dissimilarity enhancing at once its historical interest and its visible charm.   Here the eye wanders among pillars and arches which branch away in so many directions that the grandest churches can scarcely give more thoroughly the idea of infinity.   And here one stands on the site of St. Frideswide's first little church, with the very arches that she had built for her, still standing in all their primitive simplicity.   These three aisles, and the south aisle on the opposite side of the choir, are indeed eloquent of the unpretentious, lasting work that brave women have done for humanity : the latter has become, through its window, sacred to the memory of St. Catherine, whose own Latin Chapel is now for the same reason inseparably connected with St. Frideswide.   St. Cecilia looks down upon the aisle next the choir, and the chapel of Our Lady is separated from it only by the monument of the Saxon maiden, while St. Lucy has given her name to the fifth and smallest of these eastern chapels.   Thus has this great society of learned men taken pleasure in doing honour to the good women of Christendom.

The North Choir Aisle and the two aisles which adjoin it were lengthened one bay by the gradual inclusion of the eastern aisle of the transept. A heavy pier has been left with no attempt at decoration on the transept side but with a cluster of shafts on the side facing east ; and the next pier to the north has been similarly treated. It will be noticed that the arches over these western bays of the north choir aisle and Lady Chapel, being the arches of the old transept aisle, are extremely massive ; unlike anything else in the church, except the one remaining arch, is the corresponding south transept aisle (now St. Lucy's Chapel) : these are therefore thought to be unrestored parts of Ethelred's works. The fact that Norman vaulting shafts have evidently been inserted into the pier walls of the aisles point also to the conclusion that the aisle was erected at a date when vaulting shafts were not in use.

At the east end there is a small arch, extremely rough, its ragstone voussoirs patched in one part with a block of modern stone. A similar arch is to be seen in the wall of the next (Lady) Chapel, and between these two are traces of another. These three arches led to one of the most interesting architectural discoveries of recent years ; and one can hardly look at them unmoved, remembering that they form part of the original church which was built by St. Frideswide and her father. They were indeed the three " chancel arches " (if one may use the expression) which led into the three apses, the discovery of which we have described in our chapter on the exterior of the cathedral.

It was not till 1888 that the plaster was removed from the walls, and these arches exposed to view. It was then obvious that they had been part of a permanent church, and not merely temporary doorways for the convenience of Norman masons. Rough as they seem, to the expert they bear marks of care and repair, of having been, in fact, preserved as a specially venerated part of the church. As an instance of this, Mr. Park Harrison points out that one of the supporting stones is quite two feet long (longer than any other in the cathedral), and has Norman tooling upon it. It can scarcely be doubted, he says, that this was introduced to support the springing-stones of the arch, for there are clear signs that there had been some settlement. The head of the archways, too, had been plastered. In both archways there is an impost (a projection, that is, from which the arch springs), and this impost is continued through the thickness of the wall. It will be noticed that the jambs of these arches go more than two feet below the level of the floor, which is another sign of their early date. Within the apse that was reached through the southernmost archway lay the body of St. Frideswide in its first resting-place, and for long this part seems to have been held in special veneration, until the first translation in 1180, when the relics of " The Lady " were moved into a more noted place in the church, and this apse doubtless abandoned like the other two. Somewhere here the relics were then placed (as they lie to-day in the ground beneath this chapel), but the first monument has been lost. Of the second monument, which also was lost but is found again, it is now the place to speak. But, first, it may be well to explain that what is usually called the shrine of St. Frideswide is really the marble monument, or base, upon which the shrine itself formerly rested. In the Middle Ages, relics (with the two English exceptions of Westminster and St. Albans) were preserved in a shrine, usually of metal, which was enclosed in a coffer or *feretrum*.

The Shrine of St. Frideswide.—Foremost in historical interest, as well as in actual beauty, are the remains of the marble monument which have recently been put together and set up in the easternmost arch between the Lady Chapel and the north choir aisle. The coffer or shrine, which was made for the translation in 1289 (its base being therefore the most ancient monument in the cathedral), was knocked to pieces at the Reformation (1538), and, being of wood, must have entirely perished. But gradually, and from different places, fragments of the base were brought together: first, several pieces of delicately carved marble were discovered in the sides of a square well in the yard south-west of the cathedral ; then a part of the plinth on the south side was found to be in use as a step, luckily with the carved portion turned inwards ; next, a spandrel was detected by Mr. Francis, the head verger, in the wall of the cemetery ; and last of all a piece of the plinth was found in a wall in Tom Quad. Though some portions are still wanting, it is not impossible that more may yet be found.

As the monument stands now, it cannot, of course, impress one as it would have done in its perfect state, with the rich super-structure crowning it : especially as the restored shafts are merely square stone supports of the clumsiest description, so studiously careful has the restorer been not to confuse them with the original work. One cannot but applaud this con-scientious spirit (would, indeed, that it had been adopted earlier !), but at the same time the modern supports have been made quite unnecessarily hideous. Still, though the base of St. Frideswide's shrine is only a collection of fragments, these fragments are of remarkable beauty and interest. It is of Forest marble, measuring seven feet by three and a half; and consists of an arcade of two richly cusped arches at the sides and one at each end. On the top of this was fixed the *feretrum*, containing the jewelled casket that held the relics them-selves. The spandrels are filled with wonderfully carved foliage, unusually naturalistic, and preserving still the traces of colour and gilding to remind one of its former glories. The plants have been identified by Mr. Druce of High Street, the well-known Oxford botanist. On the south side there is maple in the central spandrel, with a wreath of what is probably crow's-foot in a boss below : the two side spandrels contain columbine and the greater celandine. On the north side the foliage is mostly oak, with acorns and numerous empty cups ; sycamore and ivy filling the adjoining spandrels. At the east end one of the spandrels contains vine leaves and grapes, the other fig-leaves, but without the fruit ; the cusp under the vine has a leaf which may be that of hog-leaf. At the west end there is hawthorn and bryony. The choice of all this foliage was doubtless made for symbolical reasons, referring first to St. Frideswide's life in the oak woods near Abingdon, and next to her care for the sick and suffering at Thornberrie (now Binsey). And in this connection it is pleasant to think that the sculptor, with tender fancy, chose plants which were famous for their healing virtue.

The foliage at the angles takes the form of pastoral staves ; and the intermediate spandrels at the sides have women's heads carved in the centre. The plinth, which has been set on a chamfered base and step of white stone, is ornamented with a series of quatrefoils, containing the head of a bishop at the north-west corner, and the heads of queens on the south side. Foliage, instead of a head, occupies the centre and end panels on the sides ; and very delicate foliage is worked on a little roll moulding extant at two of the angles.

Here is an account of the destruction of the shrine, and the treatment of its relics, in the words of Dean Liddell [1] :—

"It is a strange story. It is well known that, before the Reformation, the Church of St. Frideswide and her shrine enjoyed a high reputation as a place of sanctity. Privileges were conceded to it by royal authority. Miracles were believed to be wrought by a virtue attaching to it ; pilgrims from all parts resorted to it,—among the number we find the name of Queen Catherine of Aragon, whose visit to the shrine shows the veneration in which it was held. Twice a year the Vice-Chancellor and principal members of the University visited the church in solemn procession, being considered (as we are told) the 'Mother Church of University and town,—there to pray, preach, and offer oblations at her shrine.'

"These practices and privileges not unnaturally seemed to the zealous Reformers of those times to call for summary interference. The old superstitions, which certainly gave rise to many abuses, must, they thought, be abated at once ; nothing but strong measures would avail to withdraw the minds of the people, nurtured as they were in absolute belief in these superstitions, from belief in them. Accordingly, we cannot be surprised to find that this famous shrine was doomed to destruction, and was actually destroyed. When this happened it is not easy to determine,—probably in the time of Henry VIII. The fragments were used either at the time, or not long afterwards, to form part of the walls of a common well ; and there we found them. The reliques of the Saint, however, were rescued by some zealous votaries, and carefully preserved in hope of better times. Meantime Catherine (the wife of Peter Martyr, a foreign Protestant theologian of high repute, who had been appointed Regius Professor of Theology here) died, and was buried near the place lately occupied by the shrine. Over her grave sermons were preached, contrasting the pious zeal of the German Protestant with the superstitious practices that had tarnished the simplicity of the Saxon Saint. Then came another change. The Roman Church under Mary Tudor re-

[1] St. Frideswide : Two sermons preached in the Cathedral Church of Christ in Oxford, by H. G. Liddell, Dean of Christ Church, pp. 21-24.

covered a brief supremacy. The body of Peter Martyr's wife was (one regrets to learn), by order of Cardinal Pole, contemptuously cast out of the church, and the remains of St. Frideswide, preserved, as I have said, by the piety of her devotees, were restored to their former resting-place. But it does not appear that any attempt was made to restore the shrine. Party zeal still prevailed. Angry contests continued between the adherents of the two parties even after the accession of Elizabeth.

"In consequence, the Queen, soon after her accession, ordered Parker, Archbishop of Canterbury, and Grindal, Bishop of London, to look into this and other matters in dispute between the adherents of the Roman Church and those of the Reformed Faith; and these eminent ecclesiastics commissioned the authorities of this House to remove the scandal that had been caused by the inhuman treatment of Catherine Martyr's body. The matter was conducted by James Calfhill, lately appointed to a stall in this church, and then acting as sub-dean. In a letter to Bishop Grindal he gives an account of the ceremony that took place. He was resolved, if we may judge from his action, not to give a triumph to either party. On Jan. 11th, 1561, O.S., the bones of the Protestant Catherine and the Catholic St. Frideswide were put together, so intermingled that they could not be distinguished, and then placed together in the same tomb. This solution of the difficulty could not have been displeasing to the great Queen, who had been consistently endeavouring rather to win over her opponents by conciliation than to crush them by persecution. We may well suppose that she approved of the act of our Dean and Chapter. Death is the great reconciler ; enmities should, at all events, be buried with the dead."

Calfhill, the sub-dean, wrote two epigrams on the burial of Catherine Martyr with St. Frideswide. The first ends thus : *Ergo facessant hinc rabida impietas, inde superstitio ;* the other thus : *Nunc coeant pietas atque superstitio.* Perhaps these apparently contradictory sentiments led Isaac Disraeli (in his account of this curious transaction, which he selects in his "Amenities of Literature" as an illustration of the mutability of time) to remark that Calfhill "seems to have been at once a Catholic and a Reformer." Sanders the Jesuit was indignant at the "impious epithet," which he says was added, *hic jacet religio cum superstitione*; "although," says old Fuller, "the words

being capable of a favourable sense on his side, he need not
have been so angry."

The exact spot where the bones of The Lady now rest is
supposed to be marked by a brass on the floor of the Lady
Chapel, lately placed there by Canon Bright.   But we can only
be certain that, somewhere in this part of the church, "the
married nun and the virgin saint," to use Froude's words,
"were buried together, and the dust of the two still remains
under the pavement inextricably blended."

The Lady Chapel, which is the aisle next to the north
choir aisle, is sometimes called "the Dormitory," because many
of the deans are buried here : the word being a literal translation of the Greek *coemeterium* (sleeping-place), applied to the
catacombs of Rome.   It was enlarged, with the Early English
pillars and vaulting of the period, in the thirteenth century.
The shafts are filleted, and the capitals carved in the characteristic curling foliage.   It owes its position possibly to the
original dedication of the eighth century church; though the
Elder Lady Chapel of Bristol Cathedral, another Augustinian
house, is similarly situated.   Its eastern wall proves that it
must have already existed long before the thirteenth century.
The most casual observer will also be struck by the ingenuous
clumsiness with which it has been patched together.   There is
a fine Decorated four-centred window at the East End, restored
to its present condition from the mean two-light window that the
seventeenth century had made of it : underneath, at the side of
the blocked-up Saxon doorway, is a once richly coloured piscina,
the outer moulding much damaged.   The roof and arches of
the second bay from the east bears many traces of colouring,
which show among other things that the capitals were all
painted green alike, the abaci red, and the ribs of the vault
and arches red, green, and perhaps other colours.   The figures
of angels can be made out on the roof, a swinging censer being
particularly clear.   A glance from here at the high altar makes
one realise how much more bright and strong the old colour
was, and is indeed even now, than the modern.   This decoration
proves that in the second bay stood something of particular
importance.   It is generally agreed now that this was not the
shrine of St. Frideswide but the altar of Our Lady, for shrines
were placed behind and not before the altars.   Such an arrangement would leave the eastern bay of the chapel free for the

two shrines, the large one (commonly called the "Watching Chamber") and the small one recently discovered and placed opposite to it under the south-east arch. The fact that this arch is also coloured, and is the only other part which is thus treated, goes to prove that the small shrine did originally stand where it now is. Another sign is that the pillar nearest to the east end of it has been cut away, evidently to allow of a free passage round the shrine.

The Lady Chapel is divided from the Latin Chapel by four arches. Of these the first, being part of the original transept aisle, is very plain and massive, without mouldings and of one order; it springs from a square pier with shafts at the corners, and has an extremely broad soffit. It is almost beyond doubt part of Ethelred's church, and proves that the transept was finished early. The second arch is Early English, cut irregularly through the wall, which bears traces of a round arch above it. The first of the four arches which separate this chapel from the north choir aisle is similar to the one just described. The rest are very obtuse; for the two eastern bays of the Lady Chapel are two feet wider than the others, perhaps in order to increase the accommodation for worshippers at the shrine of St. Frideswide.

The "Watching Chamber."—Next in interest to the "shrine," and far more imposing in appearance, is the large tomb or watching chamber under the easternmost arch between the Lady Chapel and the Latin Chapel. Its real nature is still a matter of dispute: some maintaining it to have been used as a chantry chapel for the welfare of those who were buried below; others that it served as a "watching chamber" to protect the gold and jewels which hung about the shrine of St. Frideswide. But there is much likelihood that is was built for the new shrine of St. Frideswide, when the growing taste for elaboration in architecture tired of the comparative simplicity of the old one. If this be the case, the "watching chamber" would be in reality the third and last monument of St. Frideswide, the second being that already described, while of the first (that made for the Translation of 1180) no trace remains. The *feretrum* would have been removed from its position on the second monument, and placed within the little wooden chapel of the chamber.

Most elaborately carved and crocketed, the "watching

chamber" is a beautiful example of full-blown Perpendicular workmanship; "most lovely English work, both of heart and hand," according to Mr. Ruskin. It consists of four stories, the two lower, in stone, forming an altar tomb and canopy, and the two upper in wood. A door from the Latin Chapel leads one up a small and well-worn stone staircase into the interior of the little upper chapel, which is now a rough wooden room. Its extreme roughness suggests that it was once panelled and otherwise adorned, while there are marks at its east end, which may be the site of an altar, or of the *feretrum* itself.

The "watching chamber" belongs to the turn of the fifteenth century, and may have been erected in 1500, under the patronage of Archbishop Morton, the inventor of "Morton's fork," who died in that year, having been Chancellor of the University, and a great benefactor of it. The stone altar-tomb is of rather earlier date than the wooden superstructure, and bears the matrices of two brasses, from which one can make out enough of the horned head-dress of the female figure to settle the costume as one that remained in fashion till about 1480.

In 1889 Mr. Park Harrison explored the interior of the tomb which forms the lower portion of the "watching chamber." Entrance was effected by the removal of two steps of the staircase which leads into the Latin Chapel, and the whole space beneath the stone slab was found to be packed with carved stones and rubble. The pretty battlemented coping, which is now happily placed on the sill behind the altar of the Latin Chapel, was thus found; and also a pillar piscina of Norman date, and a fine Early English piscina, with two trefoiled arches, divided by a slender shaft with foliated cap, and profusely enriched with the tooth ornament. This latter find can now be seen lying on the slab itself.

By an accident it was discovered that what seemed to be the floor of this tomb was really the ceiling of a vault beneath. The pavement was opened in the Latin Chapel just outside the tomb, and steps were found which led to the vault through a flat four-centred doorway. In the vault was a single oak coffin, widest at the head and tapering in a straight line to the foot, like the stone coffins of an earlier period. It was apparently of fifteenth century date, and contained a body closely swathed in cerecloth; but after the coffin was opened the dust within the cerecloth rapidly subsided. The body was pronounced by experts to be that of a woman about five feet six inches in height, and was probably that of the lady in the mitred head-dress whose brass can be traced on the altar-tomb.

Monuments in the Lady Chapel.—In the bay to the west of the "watching chamber" is the tomb of *Elizabeth, Lady Montacute*, who gave to the Priory the large field now known as the Christ Church Meadow, in order to maintain two priests for her chantry in the Lady Chapel. There seems to be no ground for the statement that she built the Latin Chapel; in her foundation-deed she expressly directs the masses and other offices to be said "within the chapel of the Blessed Mary," and, so far from her bequest proving sufficient to build a new chapel, it was soon found inadequate for the

LADY MONTACUTE'S TOMB.

maintenance of the two chantry priests. Lady Montacute was the daughter of Sir Peter de Montfort, and was married first to William de Montacute, by whom she had four sons and six daughters, and afterwards to Thomas de Furnival. Her monument consists of a high tomb, the sides of which are divided into three panelled compartments. In these compartments are little statuettes of her children, and her own effigy rests on the top; at the head and foot of the tomb are quatre-foiled compartments containing sacred symbols and figures. It is very beautiful, and of great interest as showing many specimens of the costume of the period; but one can hardly imagine what its splendour must have been when the rich hues, with

which it is painted in every part, were fresh.   The colours
mentioned in the following learned description by Mr M. H.
Bloxham have long tended to monochrome, and the hand of
the mutilator has been unusually painstaking and systematic.

"The head of the effigy reposes on a double cushion, and is
supported on each side by a small figure of an angel in an alb;
these albs are loose, and not girded round the waist.   The
heads of these figures are defaced, and they are otherwise
much mutilated.   She is represented with her neck bare, her
hair disposed and confined on each side, the face within a
jewelled caul of network; over the forehead is worn a veil,
and over this is a rich cap or plaited head-dress with nébulé
folds, with a tippet attached to it and falling down behind.
Her body-dress consists of a robe or sleeveless gown, fastened
in front downwards to below the waist by a row of ornamented
buttons.   The full skirts of the gown are tastefully disposed,
but not so much so as we sometimes find on effigies of the fourteenth century.   The gown is of a red colour, flowered with
yellow and green, and at each side of the waist is an opening,
within which is disclosed the inner vest, of which the close-
fitting sleeves of the arms, extending to the wrists, form part;
this is painted of a different colour and in a different pattern
to the gown.   This was, probably the corset worn beneath the
open super-tunic.   The gown is flounced at the skirts by a
broad white border, and round the side openings, and along
the border of the top of the gown, is a rich border of leaves.
The hands, which are bare, are joined on the breast in a devo-
tional attitude.   Over the gown or super-tunic is worn the
mantle, fastened together in front of the breast by a large and
rich lozenge-shaped morse, raised in high relief.   The mantle,
of a buff colour, is covered all over with rondeaux or roundels
connected together by small bands, whilst in the intermediate
spaces are *fleur de lis*: all these are of raised work, and deserve
minute examination.   They are apparently not executed by
means of the chisel, but formed in some hard paste or composition [*gesso*] laid upon the sculptured stone and impressed
with a stamp.   The feet of the effigy appear from beneath the
skirts of the gown in black shoes, and rest against a dog."

Of the statuettes on each side of Lady Montacute's tomb,
which are each a foot and a half high, Mr Bloxham says :—
"The first and easternmost of these, on the north side, is the

most puzzling and difficult of all to describe, as regards the costume, and the more so from the mutilated state in which it now appears. It is that of a male, who is habited in a red cloak, the borders of which are jagged. This is buttoned in front to the waist by lozenge-shaped morses, and may have been the garment called the Courtepye, and discloses a short white tunic or vest, plaited in vertical folds, with a bawdrick round the body at the hips."

"Next to this is the effigy in relief of an abbess, in a long loose white gown or robe, a black mantle over, connected in front of the breast by a chain, with a tippet of the same colour. The head has been destroyed, but remains of the plaited wimple which covered the neck in front are visible, as also of the white veil on each shoulder. The pastoral staff appears on the left side, but the crook is gone.

"Two daughters of Lady Montacute were in succession Abbess of Barking, in Essex, and so, next to the last figure is another abbess similarly dressed, with the exception that the left sleeve of the gown, which is large and wide, is seen, as well as the close sleeve of the inner robe. Sculptured figures of abbesses, especially of this period, are extremely rare.

"The next figure is that of a female, in a green high-bodied gown or robe, with small pocket-holes in front and sleeves reaching only to the elbows. The fifth figure is also that of a female, in a white robe or gown, with close sleeves, close fitting to the waist, where it is belted round by a narrow girdle, and thence falls in loose folds to the feet; over this is a black mantle. There are also indications of a plaited wimple about the neck, but the head of this, as of the other effigies, has been destroyed.

"On the south side, the easternmost figure, of which the mere torso remains, is that of a male in a doublet, jagged at the skirts, and buttoned down in front from the neck to the skirts, with close sleeves buttoned from the elbows to the wrists,—*manicae botonatae*, with a bawdrick round the hips, and buckled on the right side. From the bawdrick on the left side the gipciere is suspended. This much mutilated effigy presents a good specimen of the early doublet.

"Next to it is the figure of a male, in a long red coat or gown, the *toga talaris*, with a cloak over, buttoned in front downwards from the neck as far as the third button, from

whence it is open to the skirts. This dress, in the phrase of
the fourteenth century, would be described as *cota et cloca*. In
the right hand is held a purse.

"Next to this is the figure of a Bishop, intended possibly to
represent Simon, Bishop of Ely, 1337–1344, one of the sons
of Lady Montacute. He appears in his episcopal vestments,
a white alb, with the apparel in front of the skirt, a black
dalmatica fringed and open at the sides, and a chocolate-
coloured chesible, with orfreys round the border and disposed
in front pall-wise. The parures or apparels of the amice give
it a stiff and collar-like appearance. The head of this effigy
has been destroyed, and the outline of the mitre is only visible.
The pastoral staff has been destroyed, with the exception of the
pointed ferrule with which it was shod. It was, however, held
by the left hand. The maniple is suspended from the left
arm, but no traces of the stole are visible. In more than one
instance we may notice on episcopal effigies the absence of
either the tunic or dalmatica, and sometimes of the stole.

"The fourth figure is that of a lady in a gown or robe
buttoned down in front from the breast to the waist, and with
sleeves reaching only to the elbows, from whence depend long
white liripipes or false hanging sleeves ; small pocket holes are
visible in front. From beneath this gown or super-tunic the
loose skirts of the under robe, of which also the close-fitting
sleeves are visible, appear. Behind this figure are the remains
of a mantle. The fifth and last figure is also that of a female
in a gown or super-tunic, close-fitting, and buttoned in front to
the waist."

The quatrefoiled compartments at the ends of the tomb are
particularly good : they contain,—at the head, the Blessed Virgin,
and Child, between a winged figure at a desk and an eagle,
which are the symbols of St. Matthew and St. John the Evangelist,.
—at the foot, the symbols of SS. Mark and Luke, and between
them a woman in gown and mantle with long flowing hair,
probably St. Mary Magdalene. The shields in the panels are
blazoned with the arms of Montacute, Furnival, and Montfort.

On a pillar near Lady Montacute's tomb there are two
brasses ; one bearing a graceful kneeling figure of *Johañ,*
Bishop filii Geo. Bishop, who died March 23rd, 1588 ; the
other of Thomas Thornton, who died August 17th, 1613.

The next tomb to the west of Lady Montacute is that of a

Prior, supposed to be *Alexander de Sutton*, prior from 1294 to 1316. It used to be called Guimond's tomb, and Prior Philip's, but it cannot, of course, be of their time : for the beautiful canopy, supported by Purbeck shafts with vine-leaf capitals, and powdered with ball-flower without, and groined within, as well as the figure beneath it, are Decorated, and belong to the reign of Edward I., about a hundred and fifty years later than Guimond's death in 1141. There were formerly figures at the angles, of which one on the north-west remains with a little of its original colour. The effigy, also of Purbeck marble, is thus described by Mr. M. H. Bloxham :—"The head of the effigy, which is bare and tonsured, with flowing locks by the sides of the face, reposes on a double cushion. The Prior is represented vested, with the amice about his neck with the apparel ;

ORNAMENT FROM A TOMB IN CHRIST CHURCH.

in the alb, the apparels of which appear at the skirt in front and round the close-fitting sleeves at the wrists ; with the stole, and dalmatica or tunic—which, it is somewhat difficult to say : these two latter are not sculptured, but merely painted on the effigy, and are only apparent on a careful examination ; over these is worn the chesible. This vestment is very rich, and ornamented with orfreys round the borders, over the shoulders, and straight down in front. Hanging down from the left arm is the maniple. The boots are pointed at the toes, and the feet rest against a lion. There is no indication of the pastoral staff; the hands are joined on the breast." Another proof of its fourteenth century date is that the face is close-shaven : had it been an effigy of the twelfth century the face would have been bearded.

West of this is the tomb of *Sir George Nowers* (de Nodariis), who died in 1425. His effigy gives one a good idea of the armour of his time—or rather of a period slightly before his death. Mr. Bloxham, who devoted special attention to these three monuments, thus describes the armour :—

"On the head is a conical basinet attached by a lace down the sides of the face to a camail or tippet of mail, which covers the head and shoulders, epaulières, rere, and vambraces, and coudes incase the shoulders, arms, and elbows, and on the hands are gauntlets of plate. The body-armour is covered with an emblazoned jupon, with an ornamental border of leaves, and round this, about the hips, is a rich horizontally disposed bawdrick. Beneath the jupon, which is charged with the bearing—three garbs Or—is seen the skirt or apron of mail. The thighs, knees, legs, and feet are incased in and protected by cuisses, genouillères, jambs, and sollerets, the latter composed of movable laminæ or plates, and rounded at the toes. The feet of this effigy rest against a collared dog, and the head reposes on a tilting helm, surmounted by a bull's head as a crest." On a scutcheon at the head of the tomb are the knight's arms : they are—a fess between three garbs, impaling a chevron between three greyhounds.

On the pier at the foot. of Sir George Nowers' tomb is fixed the remarkably characteristic monument of *Robert Burton*, the famous author of "The Anatomy of Melancholy," who died in 1639, having been Student of Christ Church for forty years, and also Vicar of St. Thomas', Oxford. His bust is coloured, and surrounded by an oval frame ; it should be a good likeness, and one fancies that the face is drenched in melancholy.

On the frame are two medallions with a sphere, and a curious calculation of his nativity, composed by himself, and placed here by his brother William, the historian of Leicestershire. The inscription, written by himself, is :—

> *Paucis notus, paucioribus ignotus*
> *Hic jacet*
> *Democritus Junior*
> *Cui vitam dedit et mortem*
> *Melancholia.*

At the south side of the Montacute tomb there is a stone in the floor with a large cross upon it, and an inscription in Lombardic characters of which these words can be made out :—

Johan : de : col . . . v. le : gist : ici : Dieu : . . . . . Merci.
Pour : lame : prier : dis : jours : de : pardon : aver : amen.

In the north aisle of the choir a stone commemorates *Andreas de Soltre quondam rector Ecclesiae de Kalleyn ;* and a brass, James Coorthoppe, Canon of Christ Church 1546, and Dean of Peterborough till his death in 1557. On the floor of this aisle there is also a small brass with the figure of a youth, with the Courtenay arms, and this inscription :—*Hic jacet Edvardus Courtenay, filius Hugonis Courtenay, filii Comitis Devoniæ, cujus animæ propicietur Deus.* This Hugh Courtenay, the father of the lad, must have been either Hugh second Earl of Devon, or his son Hugh, surnamed *le Fitz,* one of the heroes of Crécy.

Glass in the Aisles.—The three lovely east windows of the aisles and Lady Chapel were designed by Sir Edward Burne-Jones and executed by Mr. William Morris. The only possible criticism is that made by Mr. Ruskin, who once said that they were beautiful pictures, but were they windows ? They are perhaps open to the objection, but a comparison of them with the Reynolds windows in New College Chapel, which are flagrant offenders in this way, makes one feel that the objection is purely formal, and that these are true windows, adding colour and interest to the old cathedral in a perfectly legitimate way. One is naturally prejudiced against large figures pictorially treated, because of the atrocities of the Munich school, but these were made, not at Munich but at Merton, by the most accomplished craftsman of the century.

The first window, that in the Lady Chapel, was erected in memory of Frederick Vyner, an undergraduate of the House, who was murdered by brigands at Marathon in 1870. The figures represent. Samuel the Prophet, David, King of Israel, John the Evangelist, and Timothy the Bishop. In the panels beneath are, Eli instructing the young Samuel, David slaying Goliath, St. John at the last supper, and Timothy as a little boy learning from his mother. The legends are :—(1) *Loquere Domine, quia audit servus tuus,* and in the panel *Prope est Dominus quibus invocantibus eum ;* (2) *Deus, Deus, meus, ad te de luce vigilo,* and *Tua est Domine victoria ;* (3) *Qui recubit in· coena super pectus ejus,* and *Quis nos separabit a charitate Christi ;* (4) *Dabit tibi Dominus in omnibus intellectum,* and *Statuit super petram pedes meos.*

H

At the end of the north choir aisle is the St. Cecilia window, presented in honour of the patroness of music by Dr. Corfe, a former organist, in 1873. In the centre light the saint is represented playing her regal or small hand-organ; two angels holding other musical instruments, with palms in their hands, stand by her. The drapery is wrought in white glass, the angels have pale blue wings, and the flesh tints matted over with red tell warm against the drapery. In the lower panels are three scenes from her life: "Here St. Cecilia teaches her husband," "Here an angel of the Lord teaches St. Cecilia," "Here St. Cecilia wins a heavenly crown;" the saint's figure in this last panel is most touchingly drawn. These lower panels are richer in colour than the rest, and a greater variety of tints is introduced; but the colours are so delicate, and so skilfully blended, that they fall in most harmoniously with the main parts of the window. As the neighbouring window just described is full of the robust strength of manhood, so this one, in colour as well as in design, is graceful, delicate, and feminine. Probably it will lead to the north choir aisle being known by the name of St. Cecilia, whose art has certainly many votaries in Oxford. Mr. Malcolm Bell, in his monograph on Burne-Jones, gives the following description of the St. Cecilia window:—

"A still more beautiful instance of the use of simple figures with complicated draperies is found in the lovely St. Cecilia window, executed in 1874-5, a companion to the 'St. Catherine,' executed in 1878, in Christ Church Cathedral at Oxford, in which, moreover, it is enhanced by the soberness of the colouring, which, with the exception of a few touches of stronger hues in the lower panels, is green, and white, and gold, symbolic of the lily of heaven, into which mediæval commentators tortured the meaning of her name. The saint herself stands in the middle, with attendant angels on either side, bearing the palm of martyrdom, who hush their harmony while she plays. Below the left-hand angel, St. Cecilia, seated on her bed, reads to her husband Valirian the lesson of chastity. In the centre the angel brings to them the miraculous proof of the justification of her faith which he demanded from her:

> " Valirian goth home, and fint Cecilie
> Withinne his chaumbre with an aungel stonde,
> This aungel had of roses and of lillie
> Corounes two, the which he bar in honde.

THE "ST. CECILIA" WINDOW.   BY SIR EDWARD BURNE-JONES.

"The lilies, symbolical of virgin purity; the roses, of victory over death. In the third, the executioner holds her by one hand as she kneels on the floor of her bath-room, which is seen in the background, the steam still rising in it after the ineffectual attempt to roast her to death. With his sword raised he is about to strike the first of the three blows which failed to cut off her head.

> " And for ther was that tyme an ordinaunce
> That no man sholde do man such penaunce
> The ferthe stroke to smyten, softe or sore,
> This tormentour durste do no more."

At the end of the south choir aisle is the third figure window of Burne-Jones. It is dedicated to St. Catherine, and is in memory of Edith Liddell, a daughter of the late Dean, "who, having been scarcely five days betrothed, seized by a sudden attack of illness, rendered her spirit to God, June 26th, 1876." St. Catherine, crowned, is the central figure: she is painted in the likeness of Edith Liddell. On the right is the Angel of Suffering and Submission, with mutilated hands, the wheel of torture and flames beneath; on the left is the Angel of Deliverance, crushing the wheel of torture and scattering the flames. The draperies are white, the wings of the angels are a pale blue, and the curtains hanging at the back of the figures of a rich greenish blue, while the detailed background is cut out of violet-coloured glass, a daring but thoroughly successful arrangement. In the tracery above are angels playing triumphant music. The whole is as beautifully executed as it is finely conceived. In the three lower panels are scenes from the life and death of the saint :—(1) She disputes with philosophers, pleading for her fellow Christians, and demonstrating *avec force syllogismes* the truth of Christianity, and the falsity of paganism. This little panel has as large an effect as if it were a fresco covering half a wall. (2) Her dream, in which she is led through a wilderness by the blessed Virgin into the presence of our Lord, who is seated amid a concourse of cherubim. The way in which the cherubim are cut out of tones of ruby, full of depth, and without a suspicion of crudeness, should be noticed, and compared with the treatment of ruby glass elsewhere. This is perhaps the most beautifully drawn picture of all; and the figure of St. Mary is something not to be forgotten. (3) St. Catherine is laid in the tomb by angels. The inscriptions are :—*Agnus reget illos, et deducet eos ad vitae fontes aquarum, et absterget Deus omnem lachrymam ab oculis eorum. Timor Domini ipsa est sapientia. Beati mundo corde quoniam Deum videbunt. Cum dederit dilectis suis somnum.*

The two first windows in the wall of the south choir aisle, in memory of Dr. Jelf, Canon from 1830–1871, are by Hardman. Next is a most interesting glass painting of Bishop King, last abbot of Oseney, and first Bishop of Oxford, which is perhaps from the hand of Van Ling. This window, with some others, was taken down during the Civil War, buried for safety by a member of the family, and put up again at the Restoration. The Bishop is represented standing vested in a jewelled cope of cloth of gold, and mitre, a pastoral staff in his gloved hand. In the background, among the trees, is a picture of Oseney Abbey in its already ruined condition (c. 1630), drawn without much feeling for its architecture, but of great value as almost the only picture of the place we possess. The western tower was the first home of what are now the Christ Church bells. Three coats of arms (being those of the Bishop, impaled with the abbey of Oseney and the see of Oxford) complete the richness of what is a very good example of seventeenth century *painted* glass, in the strict sense of the word.

It is to be regretted that some of the glass, which formerly was seen by everybody in the cathedral, has been removed to the chapter-house, where it is seen by few : among the glass thus removed the lovely I.H.C. should not be missed.

The Latin Chapel (St. Catherine's, or the Divinity Chapel, St. Catherine being the patroness of students in theology) was built on to the rest in two parts, the walls of the Lady Chapel being cut into arches, and duly fitted with shafts. The first bay from the west is, like that of the Lady Chapel, part of the transept aisle ; the second bay was built in the thirteenth century, so as to form a chapel like that of St. Lucy on the south side of the church ; the third and fourth were added in the fourteenth century, and make now one large chapel, very secluded and self-contained, a kind of *hortus inclusus* that has an attraction peculiarly its own, and dwells pleasantly in the memory of every one who sees it. It is that supremely excellent thing, a church within a church,

without which no cathedral can be what its builders intended
it to be; nor any religious building fulfil that instinctive
desire of men for an inner place, where they can find their
way to the inner places of their own hearts. In such a home
of recollectedness, doubly guarded against the dogging world
without, is "rest without languor and recreation without excite-
ment"; in such a place one is "never less alone than when
alone"; and the fine sympathy with the needs of workaday
humanity, which led mediæval archi-
tects to build such sanctuaries as this
chapel here, or the Lady Chapel of so
many churches, had led men in far
earlier ages to find room even within
the travelling tabernacle of a wandering tribe for a holy place and a holy
of holies. Such being the case, it was
like the crude instincts of the "dark
ages of architecture" to choose this
very chapel as most suitable for a
lecture-hall—out of all the lofty rooms
in the spacious college. Quite lately

WINDOW IN THE LATIN
CHAPEL.

this practice has been dropped, and the Latin Chapel restored
to something of its ancient sanctity, though a good deal remains
to be done in a place where there is not as yet even a chair to
proclaim a *siste viator*.

The Decorated vaulting was built when the chapel was enlarged in the fourteenth century. The foliage of its bosses is
very beautiful; the water-lilies especially of the third boss, so
suggestive of Oxford streams, and the roses a little further
east, are a happy combination of naturalistic treatment with
decorative restraint. It will be noticed that the vaulting does
not run true in the third bay, the Decorated work there having
been somewhat awkwardly joined to the Early English of the
second bay. That part of the old wall which forms the pier
at the juncture has been left in a strangely rough condition;
the builder having seemingly given up the problem of fitting
the vaults to the unequal spaces of the bays, and left the pier
as a simple bit of old wall, without even a moulding to mark
its juncture with the vault.

A prominent feature in the Latin Chapel is the old oak
stalling, which a second inspection proves to be patchwork.

The returned stalls at the west end probably belonged to the choir of the conventual church, and in that case would have been fitted in here when Dean Duppa "adorned" the choir by destroying the old wood-work. Near to these is some of the work prepared for Cardinal Wolsey's new chapel. The poppy-heads are good specimens of wood-carving, and contain a monogram I.H.S., a heart in a crown of thorns, a cardinal's hat, and other devices. The pulpit, with its delicate canopy, an excellent specimen of seventeenth century wood-work, was formerly the Vice-Chancellor's seat in another part of the church, occupied by him during university sermons. It was then used by the Regius Professor of Divinity for his lectures, but since the altar was restored six years ago, the chapel has been no longer used as a lecture room. At the time when it was refitted, a handsome ogival arch was found in the wall near the north end of the altar : the moulding is deeply re-cessed, and once the arch terminated in what must have been an ornate finial. The top of this finial has been cut down to a level with the window ledge, and the face of the moulding hacked off to make the wall flat for the panelling, which has now been removed. It was probably the "Easter Sepulchre," where the Host was deposited on Good Friday, but it may have been the tomb of the founder of the chapel. The curious break in the masonry at the back has not been yet explained.

The wall behind the altar is pleasantly hung with Morris velvet. The altar itself was the high altar before the restoration of 1870. In 1890 new legs were made for it out of the old organ screen, and it was placed in its present position.

The eastern window (inserted as a memorial to Canon Bull) is a pathetic instance of the corrupt following of Mr. Ruskin, which also inflicted upon Christ Church the gaunt Meadow Buildings. It is, of course, really as unlike Mr. Ruskin's well-loved Venetian work as anything can possibly be : as heavy as that is light, as clumsy as that is graceful, it is ugly and cold and dead ; ·but it represents a genuine enthusiasm of the fifties, and commands our respect as an honest though mis-taken effort, a landmark in the history of the architectural revival. It also illustrates a truth which one is apt sometimes to forget,—that it is easy to appreciate beauty, and very hard to create it.

Fortunately it is nearly lost sight of in the splendid Burne-

Jones glass which fills it, and represents another side of the artistic revival not less important than the architectural.

Glass in Latin Chapel.—The beautiful windows at the side are filled with fine fourteenth century glass, which was replaced after a long period of exile by Dean Liddell. In the middle of each light is a figure in canopy work, the rest of the light being covered with " quarries,"—that is, diamond-shaped pieces of glass with leaves and flowers lightly burnt upon them. The spaces in the tracery are ornamented with curious medallions, and the borders with various beasts, as in St. Lucy's Chapel, monkeys among them. The Courtenay Arms—Three Torteaux—suggest that the family may have contributed towards building the chapel. Beginning at the west, the first window contains a St. Catherine in the first light, next a Madonna and holy Child (the blue pattern at the back of these figures should be noticed) ; next a figure of St. Frideswide, or her mother Saffrida.

The second window contains the figure of an archbishop, holding a cross curiously blended into a crooked pastoral staff ; angels are on either side.

The next has St. Frideswide in the centre, with St. Margaret and St. Catherine at her side. The patroness holds the curiously foliated sceptre which has led to the identification of her figure in the choir boss, and Catherine handles her wheel and sword in the same way as her statue over the dean's stall in the choir. The last window on this side is by Clayton and Bell, and a particularly feeble one.

The St. Frideswide window at the east end of the Latin Chapel was designed by Sir E. Burne-Jones and executed by Messrs. Powell of the Whitefriars Glass Works, the firm which is now making the glass for the mosaics at St. Paul's. " Burne-Jones, an Oxford undergraduate, destined for the Church, but gifted with high powers of romantic design, sought out Rossetti towards June 1856, and showed him some drawings. Rossetti told him at once that he ought to be, and must be, an artist, and he became one." In the next year Rossetti drew the attention of the Powells to the young artist, and they had the penetration to recognise his worth and to employ him. But though this is one of the first windows that Burne-Jones ever designed, it is one of his best. Better suited (as many think) to the purpose of a window, at all events in this enclosed chapel, than the freer method of the other glass, it carries on the best traditions of the craft, in its infinite variety of gem-like colour and complexity of detail; while it attains a degree of perfection in pictorial effect and figure-drawing which was impossible during the great era of mediæval glass-painting. The death of the saint, with its lovely effect of light through the latticed window, for instance, and the picture of her in the pig-sty, would be perfect as finished pictures, and yet do not for an instant outstep the convention which is necessary for their function as part of a window. The fact that the subjects are a little crowded is not the artist's fault. Mr. Woodward, the architect to whom the commission was due, made an unlucky mistake about the measurements, being in very ill-health at the time, and indeed on the point of death. Mr. Burne-Jones' cartoon had therefore to undergo a mechanical reduction which has slightly affected the clearness of the designs. The colour is, in spite (or rather because) of its radiant variety, not so immediately attractive to everyone as that of the other Burne-Jones windows; but when one has sat down for five or ten minutes and deciphered the various scenes, its unapproach-able beauty becomes apparent, and each succeeding visit deepens the impression of the splendour and poetry of this incomparable work.

The scenes depicted are, by the artist's own account, as follows :—

First Light.

St. Frideswide and her companions brought up by St. Cecilia and St. Catherine.
St. Frideswide founds her first convent.
A messenger from the King of Mercia demands her in marriage.
The King comes to take her by force, and the first convent is broken up.

Second Light.

Flight of St. Frideswide to Abingdon.
The King of Mercia and his soldiers in pursuit.
The Flight continued.
The Pursuit continued.
St. Frideswide takes refuge in a pig-sty.

Third Light.

Flight of St. Frideswide to Binsey.
The King of Mercia in pursuit.
St. Frideswide founds a new convent at Binsey.
Her merciful deeds.

SECTION OF TOWER, WITH A COMPARTMENT OF BAY AND CHOIR,
BEFORE THE RESTORATIONS (*Britton*).

Fourth Light.

Return of St. Frideswide to Oxford.
The Siege of Oxford by the King of Mercia.
The Siege continued.
The King struck blind.
The Death of St. Frideswide.

In the tracery above are the trees of life and of knowledge, and a ship of souls convoyed by angels.

This east window was purchased with money left by Dr. Bull (1853), to whom there is a monument against the western wall. There are also brasses to the eminent Dr. Mozley (Regius Professor of Divinity till 1878), Dr. Ogilvie (1873), Dr. Shirley (1866), Dr Barnes (1859), Archdeacon Clerke (1877).

CHAPTER IV.

ST. FRIDESWIDE (Fritheswithe, " The Bond of Peace "), found-
ress and patron saint of the church, lived early in the eighth
century, when Ethelbald was King of Mercia. Her father
Didan was probably the under-king of the little town of Oxford,
which was then a frontier city of Mercia. In spite of the legendary atmosphere that has gathered about her memory, there
is no reason to doubt the main facts of her life ; indeed, the
best modern authorities endorse them.

Here is her story, told in the delightful words of Anthony
a Wood, who wrote towards the end of the seventeenth century : —

"About the year of our Lord 727, as authors say, lived in
the city of Oxford a prince (or as Malmesbury hath, a king)
named Didan, one of incomparable honesty and virtues, who,
by his wife Safrid, of a Saxon family, had an only daughter
called Frideswyde, born at this place, and by her parents brought
up in all·manner of honest and liberal breeding, befitting her
descent." Then is described her early piety, her refusal of
marriage, and her refusal also to be a nun. The narrative
continues :—

"And furthermore, with great zeale, she added that seeing
he had large possessions and inheritances and that she was
like to enjoy most of them after his discease, he could not doe
better than bestowe them upon some religious fabrick wherein
she and her spirituall sisters (votaresses also) might spend their
dayes in prayers and singing of psalmes and hymmes to God.
To which the father giving an attentive eare and considering
withall that his issue was like to be discontinued, took upon
him a resolution to performe the same that soe he might leave

rage against "that witch, hagge, and fury Frideswyde," and
planned vengeance :—"The king then gathering a force and
intending for Oxon, breathed out nothing but fire and sword
to this place.   But the night before he came hither, there was
an angel (as the story goes) appeared to Frideswyde in a dreame,
saying to her these words : '*Ignoras, O Virgo,*' &c.: 'thou art
as yet ignorant, O virgin, what will befall you to-morrow : for
King Algar with his assistants intend to sett upon you and if it
be possible will satisfy his lust upon you and leave you a
miserable creature.   But doe not feare : there is a safe place
provided for you ; and he for this his attempt shall be struck
blind and never recover his sight. · Arise therefore, and make
hast to the way that leads to the river Thames, where you shall
find a ship boat ready provided for you and one in it to convey
you away in safety.'   After this was pronounced Frideswyde
awakened ; and, suddenly arising from her couch, took two of
her sisters the nunns named Katherine and Cicely; and
walked to the place appointed her by the angell in her
dreame.   Where according to his admonitions, she found a
boat by the river's side and in it the appearance of a yong
man with a beautiful countenance and clothed in white : who,
mitigating their feare with pleasant speech, placed them in the
boat, in which, the space of one hour, shee and her sisters
arrived neare the towne called Benton [Bampton or Bensington],
ten miles and above distant from Oxon.

   " Where after their landing, followed a path adjoyning, which
conveyed them into a vast and dismall wood.   And wandring
therin too and fro, met at length with a kind of hovell or
shelter purposely erected to harbour swine and other cattell in
times of cold and wett weather ; and there taking up a resolution to fix, crossed themselves and retired therin.   Which place
being quickly overgrowen with ivy and other sprouts, they
continued therin a long time, being in fasting and prayers, and
utterly unknown to the inhabitants therabouts."

   Algar in the meanwhile had gone to Oxford, found Frideswide
flown, and in the midst of his fury been smitten with blindness.
After living three years in close retirement in the Benton wood,
Frideswide, to comfort the nuns whom she had left, came by
boat to Binsey near Oxford, and there lived for some time.
Soon after she came back into Oxford, and spent her days in
the service of the people, working in especial many miracles of

unless it was by a forced stealth.   These were his last thoughts ;
and this he was resolved to prosecute.

"Wherefore, immediately summoning some of his faithfull
servants, sent them as embassadours to profer (under pretence)
his last desires for marriage, with full power, if like to prosper,
to complete it.   With this speciall and soveiraign caution, if
she did not concede, to watch their opportunity and carry her
away by force."

Then follows the account of the visit of the ambassadors,
their threats of force, and the Saint's undaunted reply.   The
story proceeds :—

"Well, the night is spent in consultation, and at the dawning
of the day they sallied from their lodgings and made their
appearance towards the, Nunnery, where clambering the fences.
of the house and by degrees approching her private lodging
promised to themselves nothing but surety of their prize.   But
alas ! their purposes came short.   What shall we think the
event of this designe ?   Why ! their hopes were utterly frustrated.
For shee, either by the noise they made at their entrance or
else (as 'tis said in another place) by the instinct of some good
spirit, awakened and suddenly arose to see what was the matter.
And immediately discovering who they were and their intent
for what they came, and finding it in vaine to make an escape
from them by flight being soe closely beseiged, she (as the best
remidy) straightway prostrated her selfe flatt on her face and
fervently prayed to the almighty that·he would præserve her
from the violence of those wicked persons that were now ready
to take her away, that he would show some speciall token of
reveng upon them for this their bold attempt.   Wherefore the
embassadors (as 'tis delivered) were miraculously struck blind,
and like mad men ran headlong yelling about the city."

The townsmen were much amazed at this strange sight, and
—"Upon this the cheifest of them went straightway to her and
falling upon their knees, humbly desired her to grant those
simple and impertinent people their sights, promising withall
that, as sone as they were perfected, would see them out of
towne and enjoyne them noe more to returne.   Hereupon she
commanded them to be brought to her ; and after fervent
prayers in their behalfe, were as wonderfully restored to their
eyes againe, as before they were deprived of them."

On the ambassadors' return to Algar, he was filled with

"Some time," says Dugdale, "after the glorious death of St. Frideswide, the nuns having been taken away, Secular Canons were introduced." We cannot fix the date when the community of nuns which the saint had founded was thus removed, but the passage which follows in Dugdale makes it clear that the seculars were in possession in 1004, when Ethelred II. rebuilt the church. It seems strange that the nuns, for whom Frideswide had suffered so much and laboured so successfully, should have been thus early made to give place to a chapter of married priests; but early it must have been, for by the middle of the tenth century Dunstan was busy suppressing the seculars, and enforcing everywhere the stricter monastic rule. Nor did the nuns ever come back; for, when the Secular Canons had finally disappeared, by the time of the Norman Conquest, the priory, after being for a long time in ruins, was made over, first to the great Benedictine monastery of Abingdon, of which it became a "cell" or dependency, shortly afterwards to the warlike Roger, Bishop of Salisbury, " but only for the profits issuing from their lands, which he, after its restoration, returned again with great reluctancy"; and it was finally restored under Henry I. (1111) as a house of the Canons Regular of St. Augustine, an order holding a position midway between monks and secular canons, in whose hands it continued henceforward.

Guimond was the first prior, and a curious story is told by several old writers as to the manner whereby he won the king's favour :—

"On Rogation Sunday (30th April 1122), when the king was at mass and Guymundus performing divine service before him, did when he came to that parcell of the prophet, 'it did not rain upon the earth for the space of III. years and six months,' read thus, 'it did not rain upon the earth one, one, one years and six months.' Which the king observing, and all the clerks marvelling and laughing at, did when mass was ended reprove him for it, and furthermore asked him the reason why he read after that manner. Guymund smilingly answered, 'Because you, my liege, are used to bestow your bishopricks and other church benefices to them that read so; and therefore be it known to you, henceforth I will serve no other master but Christ my King and Sovereign, who knoweth as well how to confer temporal as eternal benefits upon his servants that always obey him.'"

By the eleventh century important national meetings were held in Oxford, as when in 1020, Cnut being then king, the English and Danes were reconciled, and both nations agreed to observe the laws of Edgar. But no king ventured to visit the city, for, after the failure of Algar, there was a tradition that boded misfortune to any king who entered within the city walls. Henry III. was the first to defy it by coming to worship at the shrine of St. Frideswide in 1264; but his example was an unfortunate one, for within six weeks Nemesis came in the Battle of Lewes. Edward I. was less daring than his father, for in 1275, when he reached the gates of Oxford, he turned his horse about, and sought a lodging outside the town. Later in his reign, however, he made the venture, and destroyed the superstition.

St. Frideswide's Priory did not, according to the latest authority on mediæval universities, Mr. Rashdall, create Oxford University,* but reasons of convenience of access and other like matter-of-fact causes; for, if the University had needed only a religious house round which to cluster, the neighbouring monastery of Abingdon was far larger and more suitable. Yet there is great probability that the first germs of the University were produced by the Priory. It is said, indeed, that the Mercian kings built inns or halls in the neighbourhood of the convent, but we may suspect this as a legendary statement not more substantiable than the story of King Alfred's founding University College, since the first actual notice of "Oxeneford" does not occur till 912. But it is much more certain that, during the wise rule of Guimond (1122-1141), the first Regular Prior, and of Robert of Cricklade,† his successor, there was a school connected with the convent, as indeed was the case with most convents, and probably with St. Frideswide's itself before Guimond's time. This school stood near

* Mr. Rashdall's theory has, however, already been called in question by Mr. A. F. Leach, who (*National Review*, September 1896) asserts decisively that there were schools at Oxford even before Guimond's time, and that "Oxford is as much, there is every reason to believe, a natural growth from the schools and schoolmasters of St. Frideswide's as Paris from those of Notre Dame."

† Prior Robert published an abridgment of Pliny, addressed "to the studious, and especially to those in cloisters and schools." He also published another work on *Jacob's Marriage*, which he said he had written when he was himself a scholar and "a regent master."

the west end of the church, about the middle of what is now
Tom Quad.   Writing of the arrival of Vacarius, in King
Stephen's reign, Mr. J. R. Green says:—"We know nothing
of the causes which drew students and teachers within the
walls of Oxford.   It is possible that here, as elsewhere, the
new teacher had quickened older educational foundations, and
that the cloisters of Osney and St. Frideswide already possessed
schools which burst into a larger life. under the impulse of
Vacarius."

The Priory was also one of the centres of university life
in its early days, occupying perhaps in some sort the position
held by St. Mary's at the present day.   From the time of the
Translation of St. Frideswide, the chancellor and scholars of
the University used to go in Mid-Lent and on Ascension Day
"in a general procession to her church, as the mother-church
of the University and town, there to pray, preach, and offer
oblations to her shrine."   The Civil Law School belonged to
St. Frideswide's as well as St. Patrick's Schools, and some
others situated near to School Street.   Among the Halls that
the Priors possessed, Brend Hall was in 1438 made over to
Lincoln College; Urban Hall and Bekes Inn were bought by
Bishop Fox to procure a site for Corpus Christi College.

Yet St. Frideswide's does not seem to have been so great
a power in educational matters as its position would have
warranted.   In fact, most of the other orders were ahead of
the Augustinian Regulars in this matter, for we do not hear of
their doing anything much until the fifteenth century, when
St. Mary's College near Northgate Street was an Augustinian
establishment.   It was the new orders, the Black Friars
(Dominicans) and the Grey Friars (Franciscans), who did so
much for the educational advance of Oxford.   The Franciscan
schoolmen, especially, gave the University a European reputation, for Roger Bacon, Duns Scotus, and William Occam
were trained by them.   Cardinal Wolsey, though he did much
harm to St. Frideswide's church, did at least make the place a
great educational centre.

In one indirect way we find that the Priory helped to attend
to the scholars' interests in the thirteenth century.   "Owing to
the general poverty," says Mr. Boase, "charitable people founded
chests, from which loans might be made to poor scholars.
Grostête began the system in 1240 by issuing an ordinance

regulating St. Frideswide's Chest, which received the fines paid by citizens ; and we hear on the whole of about two dozen of these charitable funds, amounting in all to nearly 2000 marks. The money was lent out on security of books, plate, or other property, and it was, in fact, a pawnbroking business which charged no interest." The money accruing to the University was placed in a chest at St. Frideswide's, when the borrower was required to deposit some pledge—a book or a cup, or a piece of clothing. Pledges not redeemed within a year were sold by public auction. As time went on, private bequests were added to the Frideswide chest, to the great relief, no doubt, of the scholars, who were as poor as could be.

The Fair of St. Frideswide was another useful institution connected with the Priory, for in early days the fairs not only afforded much innocent amusement, but they also served to mark the seasons of the year, and were of great practical value in the domestic economy of the people. St. Frideswide's Fair lasted for seven days, and during that time the keys of the city passed from the mayor to the prior, and the town courts were closed in favour of the Piepowder Court, held by the steward of the Priory for the redress of all disorders committed during the fair. By Stuart times the Fair had fallen almost to nothing, but its memory is still kept up by the annual cakestall in St. Aldate's.

One of the strongest Jewries in England existed in Oxford, so the chest was a useful form of charity in the days when Jews were the only money-lenders, and it was found necessary to pass a law preventing the Hebrews of Oxford from charging over 43 per cent. on loans to scholars. In 1268 St. Frideswide's provided a curious proof of the strong protection which the Jews enjoyed till their expulsion from England for four centuries in 1290.

" The feud between the Priory and the Jewry went on for a century more, till it culminated in a daring act of fanaticism on Ascension Day 1268. As the usual procession of scholars and citizens returned from St. Frideswide's, a Jew suddenly burst from the group of his friends in front of the synagogue, and snatching the crucifix from its bearer, trod it underfoot. But even in presence of such an outrage, the terror of the Crown shielded the Jewry from any burst of popular indignation. The king condemned the Jews of Oxford to make a heavy

silver crucifix for the University to carry in the processions, and
to erect a cross of marble on the spot where the crime was
committed; but even this was in part remitted, and a less
offensive place was allotted for the cross in an open plot by
Merton College." The event which had opened the feud between the Priory and the Jews happened about 1185, when
Prior Phillip complained of a certain *Deus-eum-crescat* (Gedaliah),
son of Mossey, who stood at his door as the procession of St.
Frideswide passed by, and mocked at her miracles, no one
daring to meddle with him.

An instance of the widespread fame of the shrine of St.
Frideswide, and the veneration in which it was held even
shortly before its destruction, is given in Wood's "Annals." In
1518, "Queen Katherine being desirous to come to Oxford,
was attended in her journey by the Cardinal [Wolsey] : and being
entered within the limits, was received by the scholars with all
demonstrations of love and joy. After she had received their
curtesies, she retired to St. Frideswydd Monastery to do her
devotions to the sacred reliques of that Virgin Saint, being the
chief occasion, it seems, that brought her hither."

But the great change was rapidly approaching. It had
indeed been foreshadowed nearly a century and a half before,
as when, for instance, on Ascension Day 1382, Wyclif's disciple
Nicholas Hereford, preaching in the churchyard of St. Frideswide's, made a violent attack on the Mendicant Friars, and
boldly asserted his sympathy with Wyclif.

The suppression of the Priory in 1524 was not, however, a Protestant act ; for Wolsey obtained a bull from Pope Clement VII.,
authorising him, with the royal consent, to suppress the Priory
of St. Frideswide, and to transfer the canons to other houses of
the Augustinian order, so that their dwelling and revenues
might be assigned to the proposed college of secular clerks.
Wolsey had magnificent ideas about education,—"indeed,"
says Fuller, "nothing mean could enter into this man's mind";
he was bent on founding institutions which should surpass
even those of William of Wykeham and William Waynflete ;
and he saw that monasticism had fallen into disrepute, with
no prospect of restoration to public favour. He adopted,
therefore, the hitherto exceptional method of suppressing
certain priories, in order that he might endow with their
revenues his new foundation of Cardinal College, as it was first

styled. Henry VIII. readily assented to the scheme, and his minister was thus enabled to dissolve the oldest religious establishment within the walls of Oxford, and to dispose of its income of "almost £300 a year." Dr. John Barton, the last Prior of St. Frideswide's, was elected to be Abbot of the neighbouring monastery of Oseney, just as (a little later) Bishop King, the last Abbot of Oseney, was made first Bishop of Oxford.

There was much popular opposition to Wolsey's act in suppressing St. Frideswide's, and (by a second Papal Bull) certain other monasteries. Hall, a chronicler unfriendly to Wolsey, averred that "the poor wretches" ejected from the monasteries received scarcely any compensation. Complaints such as these drew from Wolsey this earnest and redundant contradiction :—

"Almighty God I take to my record, I have not meant, intended, or gone about, ne also have willed mine officers, to do anything concerning the said suppressions, but under such form and manner as is and hath largely been to the full satisfaction, recompense, and joyous contentation of any person which hath had, or could pretend to have, right or interest in the same, in such wise that many of them, giving thanks and laud to God for the good chance succeeded unto them, would for nothing, if they might, return or be restored and put again in their former state, as your Highness shall abundantly and largely perceive at my next repairing unto the same.

" Verily, sir, I would be loth to be noted that I should intend such a virtuous foundation for the increase of your Highness' merit, profit of your subjects, the advancement of good learning, and for the weale of my poor soul, to be established or acquired *ex rapinis.*"

It was indeed, says Mr. Maxwell Lyte, part of Wolsey's " grand and statesmanlike scheme of establishing episcopal sees in some of the larger monasteries, and annexing thereto smaller monasteries to provide greater revenues." The graduates of Oxford were very grateful, and promised to remember him in their prayers to the end of time ; but great fear came over the monks. His proceedings, says Fuller quaintly but truly, "made all the forest of religious foundations in England to shake, justly fearing the king would finish to fell the oaks, seeing the Cardinal began to cut the underwood."

Thus was Cardinal College founded. Its magnificence

certainly made a great impression upon Englishmen, as is
shown by the fact that it is the only existing college mentioned by Shakespeare.   In *Henry VIII.* Wolsey is praised
for his new foundation :—

> " though unfinished, yet so famous,
> So excellent in art, and yet so rising,
> That Christendom shall ever speak his virtue."

But all Wolsey's great buildings, and projects still greater,
were stopped by his sudden fall in 1529.   Three years afterwards "bluff Harry broke into the spence," and, placidly
transferring the whole credit of the idea to himself, refounded
Cardinal College with the title " King Henry VIII. his College."
Then he suppressed his own foundation, and, on Nov. 4th,
1546, reconstituted it, adopting the novel and economical
expedient of combining a cathedral with an academic
college.   The new style was *Ecclesia Christi Cathedralis Oxon
ex fundatione Regis Henrici octavi*; so St. Frideswide's church,
which had for seven years been the chapel of Cardinal College,
and of King Henry's College for thirteen years, became at
length the Cathedral Church of Christ in Oxford, and also the
chapel of the college now at length called Christ Church, and
presided over by the Dean of the cathedral.   Ever since, the
ancient church has had a two-fold character as cathedral
church and college chapel ; and " as the Dean of Christ Church
is always present, and the Bishop of Oxford very seldom,
academic usages and appearances rather prevail over the
ecclesiastical, in a way that may have been the reverse of
satisfactory to more than one occupant of the see of Oxford."
Wolsey had contemplated establishing a hundred canons ;
but Henry reduced the number at a stroke to twelve, and then
to eight ; later they were further reduced to six, which is the
present number.   Besides the canons, dean, [and bishop,
Henry's foundation included eight petty canons or chaplains,
a gospeller and a postiller or bible-clerk, eight singing clerks,
eight choristers and their master, a schoolmaster and an usher,
an organist, sixty scholars or students, and forty "children,"
corresponding no doubt to the scholars of later days.   Soon
after, however, the whole scholastic part of the establishment
was replaced by one hundred students, who (with the one
"outcomer " of the Thurston foundation) are still nightly tolled

by the hundred and one strokes of great Tom, this being the signal for college-gates to be closed all over Oxford.

Such was the. arrangement of the new establishment, which, as the name of *Ecclesia Christi* was replaced by *Ædes Christi*, came to be called, according to the double use of the word *ædes*, both Christ *Church* and the *House.* The history of the see of Oxford, which was first set up at Oseney in 1542, will be found in another chapter.

Curiously enough, the suppression of the monasteries, and the new vigorous religious movement, did not benefit the University, in spite of the addition of Wolsey's great college ; on the contrary, the Reformation nearly emptied the University, which had already lost much of its old activity during the intellectual stagnation of the fifteenth century, so that, in Edward VI.'s reign, washerwomen took to hanging out their clothes in the schools.   Most of the halls disappeared for ever, and from that time Oxford passed out of the hands of the poor man, Christ Church as the royal college becoming the special home of the gilded youth.   The first functions of the House seem indeed to have been mainly ornamental : Henry VIII. was entertained there, public declamations were given before the University under Edward VI., Cranmer was unfrocked in the cloister under Mary.   In Queen Elizabeth's reign, as well as in the seventeenth century, Christ Church Hall was used for the performance of plays, as when in 1583 *Dido* was acted, and " there was a pleasant sight of hunters, with a full cry of a kennel of hounds, and Mercury and his descending and ascending from and to a high place.   The tempest also, wherein it rained small comfits, rose-water, and snew artificial snow, was very strange to the beholders."

The Deans in Elizabeth's time were undistinguished.   There was Martiall, who was appointed by Mary, and deprived in 1559 for his religion, " which though he had two or three times changed, yet having made himself Enemies by his indiscreet Carriage, he was obliged to go into Yorkshire " ; and there was Sampson, who was " so professed an enemy of the ceremonies of the Church of England," and of organs and vestments, that he was removed by Archbishop Parker, 1565.   But there was no one else of much note till Brian Duppa was installed in 1629.   This staunch old man left Christ Church in 1641 for the Bishopric of Salisbury, after having " adorned " the cathedral, with the mixed results we have witnessed. He was extremely generous and unselfish ; and he stuck to the king through his evil days, even sharing his imprisonment. in Carisbrooke Castle, where he is thought materially to have assisted in writing the "*Eikon Basilike.*" Duppa, Mr. Wakeman tells us, "amid many dangers had boldly found means to carry on the torch of apostolic grace, even amid the proscriptions of Cromwell."

During the troubles of the Civil War, Christ Church came in for its share of the work : in 1642 a University regiment of Cavaliers was drilled in Tom Quad, and of the hundred and one students of the House twenty became officers in the king's army. After Edgehill, Charles I. occupied Oxford, and kept his court with Prince Charles in Christ Church. On February 3rd, 1644, the king appointed a thanksgiving to be made at evensong for the taking of Cirencester by Prince Rupert the day before. The doctors were then in their red robes, the officers and men in laced buff coats and polished breastplates. "But there was no new Form of Thanksgiving said, save only that Form for the victory of Edgehill, and a very solemn anthem, with this several times repeated therein— ' Thou shalt set a Crown of pure gold upon his Head, and upon his Head shall his Crown flourish.' "

In 1646 Oxford was taken by the Roundheads, and in 1648, at the visitation of the Parliamentary officers (the Dean, Samuel Fell, being in custody), Mrs. Fell, with some other ladies, and her children, refused to walk out of the Deanery, and had to be carried out with her companions, and " deposited in the quadrangle in feminine protest against extrusion." Dean Samuel Fell, who had finished Duppa's wood and glass work in the cathedral, and built the fine staircase into the hall, died heartbroken on February 1st, 1648, "the Day he was acquainted with the murder of his Royal Master King Charles I. ": he was buried at Sunningwell, near Abingdon, with this inscription of touching brevity—*Depositum S. F. Februar.* 1648.

The use of the Latin version of the Prayer Book, and the English version as well, had ceased three months before ; but it was kept up in a house in Merton Street by three Christ Church men, one of whom was the Dean's son, John Fell, afterwards himself to become Dean and Bishop of Oxford. The intruding Dean and Chapter seem to have behaved

villainously; for, in an account given by the Chapter of 1670,.
it is stated that the entire revenues of the College had been

THE INTERIOR BEFORE THE RESTORATIONS.

exhausted by the intruders, all the unfinished work on the
north side of Tom Quad demolished, and the timbers actually

sawn down from the walls and roof to be used as firewood. Almost every part of the College was damaged in this way, and the huge expense of making the destruction good had to be borne by the new Chapter after the Restoration.

Samuel Fell's first Puritan successor in the Deanery was Reynolds, a Presbyterian who, in two years (1650), was turned out "to make room," says Browne Willis, "for that noted, canting, Independent, Time-serving Hypocrite John Owen." This Owen was himself turned out in 1659, and "retired among the Dissenters at London, and there ended his Days (preaching up Sedition in Conventicles)." He was buried in Bunhill Fields, with a portentously long epitaph, whereof one sentence may suffice as a specimen—*In illâ viribus plusquam HERCULEIS, Serpentibus tribus, ARMINIO, SOCINO, CANO, venenosa strinxit guttura.*

Reynolds was restored by the Presbyterians in 1659, but them deserting, he became Bishop of Norwich, and was succeeded at Christ Church in 1660 by Marley, who, in the same year, became a Bishop, and afterwards succeeded the tough old Duppa in the see of Winchester, 1662. John Fell, who had seen so much trouble in his father's old house, was next installed therein, in 1660. His biography will be found among the bishops.

James II. made Massey, an ex-Presbyterian convert to the Roman Church, Dean of Christ Church, and the Holy Communion was celebrated according to the Roman use every day in the House. When the king visited Oxford in 1687, he was lodged in the Deanery, and a chapel fitted up for his use. He summoned the fellows of Magdalen, who had refused to admit Bishop Parker as their president, into Christ Church Hall, and said :—"Is this your Church of England loyalty? Get you gone. Know that I, your King, will be obeyed. Go and admit the Bishop of Oxon. Let those who refuse look to it. They shall feel the whole weight of my hand." They refused, and twenty-five of them were expelled. James, by-the-way, touched for the King's Evil in the cathedral about the same time.

Aldrich, the versatile, followed in the Deanery, nothing being said of Massey in the letters patent which installed him as direct successor to John Fell. We have alluded to him more than once in this book, and his monument in the nave is mentioned in its place.

After Aldrich came Francis Atterbury in 1711, who in 1713 left Oxford to combine the rather dissimilar functions of Bishop of Rochester and Dean of Westminster. He found his way into the Tower of London in 1722, being convicted of correspondence with the Pretender.

By the eighteenth century Oxford had sunk into a state of torpor, from which it began to recover in 1807, when the first honour schools were founded; though from 1783 Dean Cyril Jackson had been doing a great work in the restoration of order and efficiency at the House. Christ Church thus bore an honourable part in the revival of learning, and gradually developed from a rich man's plesaunce into a home of learning : the names of Ruskin, Gladstone, and Pusey are typical of the great men in different walks of life that have belonged to the cathedral college in our own era. Dean Gaisford more than half a century ago did much to help on the progress ; and the long rule of his successor, Dean Liddell (1855–91), familiar to every schoolboy through his famous lexicon, covered a period of immense change both in the cathedral and in the college. Dr. Liddell is now living in retirement, his successor being Dr. Francis Paget, one of the writers in "*Lux Mundi*," and the author of some well-known volumes of addresses.

Fifty years ago it was said that Christ Church was the only cathedral in Christendom where there were neither services nor sermons for the people of the diocese. But the new life, which has since then wrought such great changes in university, cathedral, and diocese alike, has left Christ Church, if still the smallest, yet not the least important of the great centres of ecclesiastical activity.

CHAPTER V.

DOWN to our own time, Oxford remained one of the new dioceses of the English Church, having been set up by Henry VIII. by way of compensation for his confiscation of the monastic properties. Before 1542 Oxford belonged to the enormous diocese of Lincoln; but in that year the new see was created, and Robert King, the last Abbot of Oseney, was made first Bishop of Oseney, and the Bishop's stool set up in his magnificent abbey church of St. Mary.

This Abbey of Oseney, which had been founded by Robert D'Oilgi in 1129, and rebuilt in 1247, was, like St. Frideswide's, a house of Augustinian Canons, but far larger. It was, indeed, one of the finest abbeys in England, its principal cloister being as large as Tom Quad, and its church no less than 352 feet by 100, with double aisles, and twenty-four altars. Gardens and courts, and comely outbuildings, ran along the side of the river; in every corner a busy life went on among the orieled windows and high-pitched roofs, within the fretted cloister, the schools and libraries, the refectory, and the kitchen, whither a conduit brought the water from the river side. A great gate looked on to the high road; and the abbot's lodgings were so spacious that six men could walk abreast up the steps which led into his hall. Yet others were not forgotten; besides the guest-house, there was a building reserved for poor clerks.

But Henry's mania for destruction could not let the Abbey stand. In 1546 he moved the see to St. Frideswide's, reconstituting the old Priory, which Wolsey had turned into a college, as both college and cathedral. The doom of Oseney was pronounced, and in that year the demolition began.

In 1566 Agar's map represents Oseney Abbey as still standing, but roofless ; in 1644 a good deal remained, but Charles I. used the greater part to complete the fortifications of Oxford against the Cromwellians ; in 1718 the abbot's chamber and the great stone staircase were all that was left. In Dr. Johnson's time a few ruins could still be seen, of which the great man said (at a time when such sentiments were un-common)—" Sir, to look upon them fills me with indignation." At the present day the remains are almost invisible ; they consist of a portion of a building attached to the mill, a fragment of the foundations of the gateway at the end of the same building, a small portion of the wall near the great gate, a few loose fragments of masonry, and some encaustic tiles. Bishop King's window in the cathedral gives one a vague reminder of its former aspect ; and only the bells, which were transferred to Christ Church, remain intact. Thus perished the first cathedral church of the see of Oxford.

> Of it there now remains no memory
> Nor any little monument to see ;
> By which the traveller that fares that way,
> That once she was may warned be to say.

Apart from questions of vandalism, the destruction of this the first cathedral of Oxford was an egregious piece of waste and folly. Such places have been only too much needed by the University—indeed the need was felt a few years after the destruction—and vast sums have been spent in the erection of immeasurably inferior buildings. If Oseney Abbey, with its crowd of beautiful outbuildings along the water side, had been converted into a college, it would have been of immense use, and every other college now extant insignificant compared with it. Of all the headstrong and wanton actions of an irreverent age, the destruction of Oseney was one of the most wicked ; and, as the train moves into Oxford railway station, the stranger may remember that the present approach to the old city is only so hideous because the glorious old abbey has given place to a collection of gasholders, coal-heaps, railway-sidings, modern tombstones, and obscene jerry-buildings.

The diocese of Oxford now includes the deaneries of Aston, Burcester, Chipping-Norton, Cuddesden, Deddington, Dor-chester (Oxon), Henley, Whitney, Woodstock, and Oxford City.

Robert King (1542-1557), the first Bishop of Oseney and of Oxford, and the last Abbot of Oseney and of Thame, began life as a Cistercian monk.   On the conversion of his abbey into a cathedral, he continued, as bishop of the new see, to preside ; but he had already, seven years before, been raised to the episcopate, as suffragan of Lincoln, under the title (conferred by the Pope) of Bishop of Rheon in the province of Athens. He seems to have taken the Reformation pretty easily, passing through all the changes under King Henry, King Edward, and Queen Mary.   He died at an advanced age in 1557, and was buried in Christ Church Cathedral.   He left considerable riches to his nephew Phillip King, "which it seems," says Fuller, "was quickly consumed, so that John King, Bishop of London (son of Phillip), used to say he believed there was a fate in abbey money no less than in abbey land, which seldom proved fortunate, or of continuance to the owners."

After Queen Elizabeth had kept the see vacant for ten years, **Hugh Curwen** (1567-1568), a "moderate papist," according to Fuller, who had been made Archbishop of Dublin by Queen Mary, and now wished to end his days in peace, was translated to Oxford.   "Very decrepid, broken with old age and many state affairs," he died next year.   Whereupon Elizabeth kept the see vacant for twenty-one years more, "out of pure devotion to the leases, as some writers say."

John Underhill (1589), Rector of Lincoln College, and one of Queen Elizabeth's chaplains, was next appointed, "being persuaded," says Willis, "on certain considerations, to accept it in the way of a better."   But it proved "very much out of his way ; for ere the first-fruits were payed he died in great dis-content and poverty about the beginning of May 1592."

Again Elizabeth, who had already taken away some of the best estates from the bishopric, kept it in her hands the third time (1592-1604) : "who," says Willis, " constituting no bishop forty-one years of her forty-four, disposed of its income to her courtiers as she thought fit, giving whatever they had a mind to ask ; though, as some writers remark, it proved miserably fatal to them, particularly to her great favourite the Earl of Essex."

With **John Bridges** (1604-1618) commences the unbroken

succession of Bishops of Oxford. It is suggested by Fuller in
his "Worthies" that "the cause that church was so long a
widow was the want of a competent estate to prefer her"; but
at this time, Elizabeth being dead, the endowment of the see
had been increased; and henceforward occupants for it were
found. Bridges is known to history mainly from his name
appearing at the head of the title-page of the first two Marpre-
late tracts. He was then, 1587, Dean of Sarum, and had
written a temperate reply to the Puritan pamphleteers who
were pouring violent abuse upon Episcopacy. Martin Marpre-
late seized upon his book, "A Defence of the Government
Established in the Church of England," and headed the
"Epistle" and the "Epitome" with, "Oh read over D. John
Bridges, for it is a worthy worke."

John Howson (1619–1628) was a great controversialist of
the time, his four sermons against the Pope's supremacy having,
according to Fuller, "made him famous to all posterity." He
was one of the original members of Chelsea College, an institution founded by James I. "to afford divines leisure and other
conveniences to spend their time wholly in controversy."
Mercifully this terrible design soon gave way, and Chelsea
College became Chelsea Hospital. Bishop Howson was
translated to Durham in 1628, where he died at the age of
ninety-five.

Richard Corbet (1628–1632) was "a distinguished wit in
an age of wits, and a liberal man amongst a race of intolerant
partizans." But perhaps his liberality (which did not prevent
him, by-the-way, from carrying out the Laudian discipline with
a high hand) was due to his own easy way of living: for he
and his chaplain were wont to lock themselves in the wine-
cellar and be merry. He seems to have been a genial, kind,
generous, and spirited prelate; sincere and affectionate in
private life, he was, says Gilchrist, "correct, eloquent, and in-
genious as a poet." At least he was a man of character. From
1632 to 1635 he was Bishop of Norwich.

John Bancroft (1632–1641), Master of University College,
and nephew of the Archbishop of Canterbury of that name,
was a great benefactor to the see. Being a single man, he

K

devoted his money to this purpose; and besides many financial acquisitions, he built an episcopal palace at Cuddesden at the suggestion of Archbishop Laud. This palace, the first since the time of Edward VI., was finished in 1634, and burnt down ten years later by Colonel Legg, to prevent its becoming useful to the parliamentary forces. It lay in ruins till the time of Bishop Fell.

Robert Skinner (1641–1663) was translated to Oxford from Bristol. He was imprisoned in the Tower by the Puritan party, and remained in obscurity during the Commonwealth. At the Restoration, being then over seventy, he was translated to Worcester.

William Paul (1663) and **Walter Blandford** (1665) did nothing memorable.

Hon. Nathaniel Crewe (1671–1674) entered into holy orders in 1664; in the short space of five years he was Dean of Chichester, and two years after that Bishop of Oxford. He was an ambitious and restless man: in 1673 he had the boldness to perform the marriage ceremony between the Duke of York and Mary of Este, in defiance of the House of Commons. As a reward for this act, the Duke procured him the see of Durham, whither he was translated in 1674. At the Revolution, as a consequence of his political intrigues, he was excepted from the general pardon, and obliged to fly to Holland. But he afterwards made his peace; and, on the death of his elder brother, becoming Lord Crewe, he was the first man to be summoned to Parliament both as baron and bishop. He lived on till 1722.

Hon. Henry Compton (1674–1675), son of the Earl of Northampton, who died fighting by the king at Hopton Heath in 1644, was after the Restoration a cornet in the army before he took orders. He was conspicuous throughout his long life for his efforts to reconcile the dissenters with the Church of England, and for his opposition to Rome; he was the first to sign the declaration for the Prince of Orange on William's arrival in London. But at Oxford he was a bird of passage, being translated to London in 1675.

John Fell (1676–1686), the best known, and also the best
of the Bishops of Oxford, was well-fitted to restore the traditions
of the place ; for his father Samuel Fell was Dean of Christ
Church from 1637–1649, and had been elected student of the
House as far back as 1601 : thus John Fell must have had an
intimate knowledge of the traditions of Christ Church as far
back as the third interregnum of Elizabeth. A strong royalist,
Fell kept in seclusion till the Restoration, when, in 1660, he
was made Dean. He at once commenced to restore both the
discipline and the buildings of the College. On his appointment to the Bishopric, he was permitted to retain the Deanery
as well, in order "that he might better carry on his noble
designs, which were so many that they contributed to wear him
quite out and shorten his life." He employed Sir Christopher
Wren to build Tom Tower, and finished the north side of
Tom Quadrangle ; he also built a new episcopal palace upon the
ruins of the old one at Cuddesden. He founded ten exhibi-
tions, and caused the University Theatre to be erected, and
the Printing Press to be " advanced to a glory superior to any
place in Christendom." He showed exemplary care in govern-
ing his diocese, and established daily prayers at St. Martin's
(as the principal city church of Oxford) at eight in the morning
and eight at night. His most important book is the " Life of Dr.
Henry Hammond," 1660 ; he also wrote several theological
books, edited St. Cyprian's works, and produced a well-known
edition of the New Testament. He died in 1686, "having by a
most pious unspotted single life left behind him an everlasting
character," and was buried in the cathedral, where, in the ante-
chapel, there is a monument to him. There is also a beautiful
statue of him over the archway that leads past the deanery into
Peckwater Quadrangle, by Mr. Bodley.

Anthony à Wood records of him that he was "the most
zealous man of his time for the Church of England." Still
John Fell had his weak points, as this same Anthony Wood
had cause to know. For it so happened that Wood had
mentioned Hobbes, the redoubtable author of the "Leviathan,"
in terms of great admiration, in his History and Antiquities of
the University. Wood was himself a strong high-churchman, with
(it had been said) a weakness for popery ; in praising Hobbes he
therefore acted with a generosity and fairness beyond his age.
Fell, however, was not so liberal ; he considered Hobbes no

better than an atheist or a deist, and when one Peers was
employed by Wood to translate his book into Latin, Fell got
on the right side of the man, and made him alter all Wood's
praises of Hobbes to expressions of abuse.   The author of the
" Leviathan," meeting the King in Pall Mall, got leave to reply,
and hit the Bishop rather hard.   Fell retorted with an answer
that contained the famous description of Hobbes as *irritabile
illud et vanissimum Malmesburiense animal.* Wood, of course,
was furious, and the wretched Peers suffered at the hands of
the muscular old Antiquary, so that " as Peers alway cometh
off with a bloody nose or a black eye, he was a long time
afraid to goe anywhere where he might chance to meet his too
powerful adversary, for fear of another drubbing."

Samuel Parker (1686–1687) was a typical specimen
of the place-hunter of the period.   He was brought up
a strict Puritan at Northampton, and, coming to Wadham
College in 1656, when the Puritans were in power, he
distinguished himself as " one of the most godly young men
in the University," and was under the tuition of a rigid Presbyterian.   Shortly after the Restoration, however, he changed his
mind, and in 1663 he took orders, becoming " a zealous
advocate of the Church of England."   By 1686, however, he
was the creature of James II., and was forced by that monarch
upon Magdalen College, Oxford, as its President, in 1687,
in the place of the lawful President, John Hough.   At the
installation only two of the Magdalen Fellows attended ; the
porter threw down his keys, the butler had to be dismissed
because he would not scratch Hough's name from the buttery
list, no blacksmith even could be found in Oxford to force the
lock of the President's lodgings ; and the whole University,
which had suffered so much for the Stuarts, was alienated at
last.   Parker himself died very soon after, in the lodgings that
he had unlawfully occupied.   He lies buried in the ante-chapel
of Magdalen, but no monument marks his grave.   Antony
Wood intimates that he would have become a Papist, but
for his wife, who was unwilling to be parted from him ; and
he certainly wrote in defence of transubstantiation.   Still,
Parker, according to Mr. W. H. Hutton (*Social England,*
iv. 421), was by no means a despicable man.   As a philo-
sopher in his *Disputationes de Deo,* and *Censure of the*

Platonick Philosophie, as a satirist in his *Discourse of Ecclesiastical Polity,* and an ecclesiastical historian, he is eminent. "But most of all is he commended to modern thinkers by his little tract containing reasons for the abolition of the Test Act."

Timothy Hall (1688–1690), another of James II.'s creatures, was also originally a Nonconformist, but afterwards, "getting nothing," says Willis, "for his loss of a small living in Middlesex, he complied." Being a very obscure and inconsiderable person, and on no account for learning, no one took any notice of him. At the Revolution he fled from Oxford, and died "miserably poor at Hackney near London, and was buried in the church there without any memorial."

John Hough (1690–1699), the President of Magdalen whom King James had ejected, was the next bishop. He retained the Presidency during his episcopate. In 1699 he was translated to Lichfield, thence in 1717 to Worcester, where he died in 1743. He was, says Macaulay, "a man of eminent virtue and prudence, who, having borne persecution with fortitude and prosperity with meekness, having risen to high honours, and having modestly declined honours higher still, died in extreme old age, yet in full vigour of mind," fifty-six years after the eventful struggle with James.

William Talbot (1669–1715), father of Lord Chancellor Talbot, was translated to Salisbury in 1715, and to Durham in 1721.

John Potter (1715–1737), son of a linen-draper in Wakefield, wrote a well-known book on the "Antiquities of Greece." He was "a learned and exemplary divine, but of a character by no means amiable, being strongly tinctured with a kind of haughtiness and severity of manners." He became Archbishop of Canterbury in 1737.

Thomas Secker (1737–1758) came of dissenting parents, but was persuaded by the great Bishop Butler to abandon the study of medicine and to take orders in the Church. He was an estimable and able person, and in 1758 became Archbishop of Canterbury. His portrait by Sir Joshua Reynolds is at Lambeth.

John Hume (1758–1766), Bishop of Bristol 1756 : translated to Salisbury 1766.

Robert Lowth (1766–1777) was the author of a variety of works, including a "Life of William of Wykeham," and a "Short Introduction to English Grammar." His controversy with Warburton, and the "Letters" to which it gave rise, are well known. Of his "Isaiah" Philip Skelton said that "Lowth on the Prophecies of Isaiah is the best book in the world, next to the Bible." He was moved to London 1777, and he refused the Archbishopric of Canterbury.

John Butler (1777–1788) was a popular preacher and political pamphleteer ; in reward apparently for his efforts in the latter function, Lord North advanced him to see of Oxford, though he was not a university man. Translated to Hereford 1788.

Edward Smallwell (1788–1799), St. David's 1783. The first bishop since Dr. Fell to remain faithful to the diocese.

John Randolph (1799–1807), regius professor of Greek and a trustee of the British Museum, was the author of many sermons and charges. One of his last works was a report of the progress of the National School Society. Translated to Bangor 1807, and to London 1809.

Charles Moss (1807–1811) avoided translation, and died shortly in the palace at Cuddesden, and "leaving his splendid furniture for the use of his successors."

William Jackson (1812–1815) was a prominent Oxford man, being regius professor of Greek and curator of the Clarendon Press.

Hon. Henry Legge (1816–1827) was a son of the Earl of Dartmouth ; he had been Dean of Windsor, and in 1817 became Warden of All Souls, retaining the bishopric.

Charles Lloyd (1827–1829). Had he not died at the early age of forty-five, Lloyd would have played a great part in the stirring times that were in store for the Church. He was, says Mr. Gladstone, "a man of powerful talents, and of character both winning and decided." He was a Christ Church don, and had Sir R. Peel among his pupils and constant friends. Lloyd warmly supported the Roman Catholic Relief Bill in 1829. He was the first to publish the Prayer Book with red lettered rubrics.

Hon. Richard Bagot (1829–1845), translated to Bath and Wells. He graduated in 1803, and it is characteristic of his times that in 1804 he was fellow of All Souls, in 1806 rector of Leigh, and in 1807 canon of Windsor,—all within seven years of his matriculation at Christ Church. He was bishop at the time of the Oxford movement, and was reluctantly obliged to play a part in its history. He did not exactly please either side, but he behaved with great fairness and courtesy. In 1845, being ruined in health by the worry of previous years, he was translated to Bath and Wells.

Samuel Wilberforce (1845–1870), translated to Winchester. This famous bishop was the third son of William Wilberforce, the great slave emancipator. At the early age of forty he was made bishop of Oxford, and he administered the diocese with wonderful ability for a quarter of a century, guiding it through the most difficult period, when the Tractarian storm was at its height, without offending either party. His extraordinary tact and charm enabled him to perform a valuable work for the Church by binding the various sections together at a time when party-feeling ran high. He was the most accomplished preacher in the English Church, one of the foremost parliamentary orators of his day; "the most witty and genial of companions, he was the favourite of social life, and was equally irresistible in the drawing room or on the platform." As a theologian he was the inferior of his brother the Archdeacon; he wrote, however, several books, of which the best remembered are "Agathas" and "Rocky Island." He was killed by a fall from his horse when riding with Lord Granville in 1873.

John Fielder Mackarness (1870–1888) was recom-

mended to the bishopric by Mr. Gladstone, having lost his seat
in convocation through refusing to oppose the disestablishment
of the Irish Church.   He was a hard-working prelate of great
courage and independence.   When an attempt was made to
force him to take proceedings against the rector of Clewer, he
argued the case in person before the judges of the Queen's
Bench, and at last won his case on appeal.   On surrendering
to the ecclesiastical commissioners the management of the
Oxford bishopric estates, Dr. Mackarness paid them the sum
of £1729, which he estimated that he had received in excess
of his statutory income during the previous nine years.   He
had been made a fellow of Exeter College on taking his degree ;
he wrote several pamphlets, among them "A Plea for Tolera-
tion, in Answer to the 'No Popery' Cry, 1850."   He resigned,
owing to failing health, in 1888, and died in the next year.

William Stubbs, the present bishop, was translated from
Chester in 1888, being already a Student of Christ Church.
He is one of the leading historians of our time, and his Consti-
tutional History has long been the standard work upon the
subject.

ARMS OF CHRIST CHURCH.

NEILL AND COMPANY, PRINTERS, EDINBURGH.

Bell's Cathedral Series.

EDITED BY

GLEESON WHITE AND E. F. STRANGE.

In specially designed cloth cover, crown 8vo, 1s. 6d. each.

Now Ready.

CANTERBURY. By HARTLEY WITHERS. 2nd Edition, revised. 36 Illustrations.
SALISBURY. By GLEESON WHITE. 2nd Edition, revised. 50 Illustrations.
CHESTER. By CHARLES HIATT. 24 Illustrations.
ROCHESTER. By G. H. PALMER, B.A. 38 Illustrations.
OXFORD. By Rev. PERCY DEARMER, M.A. 34 Illustrations.
EXETER. By PERCY ADDLESHAW, B.A. 35 Illustrations.
WINCHESTER. By P. W. SERGEANT. 50 Illustrations.
LICHFIELD. By A. B. CLIFTON. 42 Illustrations.
NORWICH. By C. H. B. QUENNELL. 38 Illustrations.
PETERBOROUGH. By Rev. W. D. SWEETING. 51 Illustrations.
HEREFORD. By A. HUGH FISHER. 34 Illustrations.

In the Press.

LINCOLN. By A. B. KENDRICK, B.A. | GLOUCESTER. By H. L. MASSÉ.
DURHAM. By J. E. BYGATE. | YORK. By A. CLUTTON BROCK, B.A.
WELLS. By Rev. PERCY DEARMER, M.A.

Preparing.

ST DAVID'S. By PHILIP ROBSON. | WORCESTER. By E. F. STRANGE.
ELY. By T. D. ATKINSON. | SOUTHWELL. By Rev. ARTHUR DIMOCK.
CHICHESTER. CARLISLE. ST PAUL'S.
ST ALBANS. RIPON. BRISTOL.

Uniform with above Series.

BEVERLEY MINSTER. By CHARLES HIATT. [*Preparing.*

Opinions of the Press.

"For the purpose at which they aim they are admirably done, and there are few visitants to any of our noble shrines who will not enjoy their visit the better for being furnished with one of these delightful books, which can be slipped into the pocket and carried with ease, and is yet distinct and legible. . . . A volume such as that on Canterbury is exactly what we want, and on our next visit we hope to have it with us. It is thoroughly helpful, and the views of the fair city and its noble cathedral are beautiful. Both volumes, moreover, will serve more than a temporary purpose, and are trustworthy as well as delightful."—*Notes and Queries.*

"We have so frequently in these columns urged the want of cheap, well-illustrated, and well-written handbooks to our cathedrals, to take the place of the out-of-date publications of local booksellers, that we are glad to hear that they have been taken in hand by Messrs George Bell & Sons."—*St James's Gazette.*

"Visitors to the cathedral cities of England must often have felt the need of some work dealing with the history and antiquities of the city itself, and the architecture and associations of the cathedral, more portable than the elaborate monographs which have been devoted to some of them, more scholarly and satisfying than the average local guide-book, and more copious than the section devoted to them in the general guide-book of the county or district. Such a legitimate need the 'Cathedral Series' now being issued by Messrs George Bell & Sons, under the editorship of Mr

Gleeson White and Mr E. F. Strange, seems well calculated to supply. The volumes are handy in size, moderate in price, well illustrated, and written in a scholarly spirit. The history of cathedral and city is intelligently set forth and accompanied by a descriptive survey of the building in all its detail. The illustrations are copious and well selected, and the series bids fair to become an indispensable companion to the cathedral tourist in England."—*Times*.

"They are nicely produced in good type, on good paper, and contain numerous illustrations, are well written, and very cheap. We should imagine architects and students of architecture will be sure to buy the series as they appear, for they contain in brief much valuable information." *—British Architect*.

"Half the charm of this little book on Canterbury springs from the writer's recognition of the historical association ·of so majestic a building with the fortunes, destinies, and habits of the English people. . . . One admirable feature of the book is its artistic illustrations. They are both lavish and satisfactory—even when regarded with critical eyes."— *Speaker*.

"There is likely to be a large demand for these attractive handbooks." —*Globe*.

"Bell's 'Cathedral Series,' so admirably edited, is more than a description of the various English cathedrals. It will be a valuable historical record, and a work of much service also to the architect. The illustrations are well selected, and in many cases not mere bald architectural drawings but reproductions of exquisite stone fancies, touched in their treatment by fancy and guided by art."—*Star*.

"Each of them contains exactly that amount of information which the intelligent visitor, who is not a specialist, will wish to have. The disposition of the various parts is judiciously proportioned, and the style is very readable. The illustrations supply a further important feature; they are both numerous and good. A series which cannot fail to be welcomed by all who are interested in the ecclesiastical buildings of England."— *Glasgow Herald*.

"Those who, either for purposes of professional study or for a cultured recreation, find it expedient to 'do' the English cathedrals will welcome the beginning of Bell's 'Cathedral Series.' This set of books is an attempt to consult, more closely, and in greater detail than the usual guide-books do, the needs of visitors to the cathedral towns. The series cannot but prove markedly successful. In each book a business-like description is given of the fabric of the church to which the volume relates, and an interesting history of the relative diocese. The books are plentifully illustrated, and are thus made attractive as well as instructive. They cannot but prove welcome to all classes of readers interested either in English Church history or in ecclesiastical architecture."—*Scotsman*.

"A set of little books which may be described as very useful, very pretty, and very cheap . . . . and alike in the letterpress, the illustrations, and the remarkably choice binding, they are ideal guides."— *Liverpool Daily Post*.

"They have nothing in common with the almost invariably wretched local guides save portability, and their only competitors in the quality and quantity of their contents are very expensive and mostly rare works, each of a size that suggests a packing-case rather than a coat-pocket. The 'Cathedral Series' are important compilations concerning history, architecture, and biography, and quite popular enough for such as take any sincere interest in their subjects."—*Sketch*.

LONDON: GEORGE BELL AND SONS.

Trieste Publishing has a massive catalogue of classic book titles. Our aim is to provide readers with the highest quality reproductions of fiction and non-fiction literature that has stood the test of time. The many thousands of books in our collection have been sourced from libraries and private collections around the world.

The titles that Trieste Publishing has chosen to be part of the collection have been scanned to simulate the original. Our readers see the books the same way that their first readers did decades or a hundred or more years ago. Books from that period are often spoiled by imperfections that did not exist in the original. Imperfections could be in the form of blurred text, photographs, or missing pages. It is highly unlikely that this would occur with one of our books. Our extensive quality control ensures that the readers of Trieste Publishing's books will be delighted with their purchase. Our staff has thoroughly reviewed every page of all the books in the collection, repairing, or if necessary, rejecting titles that are not of the highest quality. This process ensures that the reader of one of Trieste Publishing's titles receives a volume that faithfully reproduces the original, and to the maximum degree possible, gives them the experience of owning the original work.

We pride ourselves on not only creating a pathway to an extensive reservoir of books of the finest quality, but also providing value to every one of our readers. Generally, Trieste books are purchased singly - on demand, however they may also be purchased in bulk. Readers interested in bulk purchases are invited to contact us directly to enquire about our tailored bulk rates. Email: customerservice@triestepublishing.com

You May Also Like

Hour by Hour; Or, The Christian's Daily Life

E. A. L.

ISBN: 9780649607242
Paperback: 172 pages
Dimensions: 6.14 x 0.37 x 9.21 inches
Language: eng

The Little Dream: An Allegory in Six Scenes. [1911]

John Galsworthy

ISBN: 9780649637270
Paperback: 50 pages
Dimensions: 6.14 x 0.10 x 9.21 inches
Language: eng

You May Also Like

War
Poems, 1898

California Club
& Irving M. Scott

ISBN: 9780649731213
Paperback: 160 pages
Dimensions: 6.14 x 0.34 x 9.21 inches
Language: eng

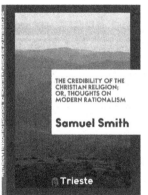

The Credibility of the Christian
Religion; Or, Thoughts
on Modern Rationalism

Samuel Smith

ISBN: 9780649557516
Paperback: 204 pages
Dimensions: 5.83 x 0.43 x 8.27 inches
Language: eng

www.triestepublishing.com

You May Also Like

1807-1907 The One Hundredth Anniversary of the incorporation of the Town of Arlington Massachusetts

Various

ISBN: 9780649420544
Paperback: 108 pages
Dimensions: 6.14 x 0.22 x 9.21 inches
Language: eng

Biennial report of the Board of State Harbor Commissioners, for the two fiscal years commencing July 1, 1890, and ending June 30, 1892

Various

ISBN: 9780649194292
Paperback: 44 pages
Dimensions: 6.14 x 0.09 x 9.21 inches
Language: eng

www.triestepublishing.com

You May Also Like

Biennial report of the Board of State Harbor Commissioners for the two fisca years. Commeneing July 1, 1884, and Ending June 30, 1886

Various

ISBN: 9780649199693
Paperback: 48 pages
Dimensions: 6.14 x 0.10 x 9.21 inches
Language: eng

Biennial report of the Board of state commissioners, for the two fiscal years, commencing July 1, 1890, and ending June 30, 1892

Various

ISBN: 9780649196395
Paperback: 44 pages
Dimensions: 6.14 x 0.09 x 9.21 inches
Language: eng

Find more of our titles on our website. We have a selection of thousands of titles that will interest you. Please visit

www.triestepublishing.com

Lightning Source UK Ltd.
Milton Keynes UK
UKOW01f1006231017
311488UK00009B/2965/P